She Was Only Three
The Trials of John Thomas James Jr.

SHE WAS ONLY 3

John D. Montgomery

Cover design by Terry Gallagher/Doowah Design Inc.

All photos courtesy of the City of Winnipeg Police Services unless otherwise noted.

Published with the generous assistance of the Manitoba Arts Council and The Canada Council for the Arts.

Printed and bound in Canada

Canadian Cataloguing in Publication Data

Montgomery, John D., 1927–
    She was only three: the trials of John Thomas James Jr.

Includes bibliographical references and index.
ISBN 1-896239-33-1
    1. James, John James—Trials, litigation, etc.
2. Trials (Murder)—Canada. 3. Juvenile justice, Administration of—Canada. I. Title.

KE229.J35M65 1998   364.15′23′0971   C98-900368-X

In Memory of Ruby

Acknowledgements

Eight long-suffering souls waded through my manuscript in its formative stages and proffered constructive criticism for which I am greatly in their debt.

Firstly, there was Garth Niven, the chief librarian of the Great Library at the old Law Courts Building in Winnipeg; then Gordon Erskine Pilkey, Q.C., a former deputy attorney general and formidable advocate.

My brother, the Honourable Robert Montgomery, one-time judge of the Supreme Court of Ontario, cautioned that I temper my treatment of certain jurists. With gratitude, I declined to heed his admonition.

To Crown attorneys Cathy Everett, Robert "Tiger" Morrison and Richard Saull, for their wise counsel, my sincere appreciation.

Joan Rose prepared the manuscript and maintained her radiant smile throughout this ordeal.

My wife Jennifer has been my main source of inspiration as well as my thirteenth juror throughout the years.

The aforementioned have my grateful thanks.

J.D.M.
March 1998

Table of Contents

Preface

This is the true story of the apprehension and conviction of a sadistic and unrepentant killer. It is, as well, a true account of a decaying criminal justice system in which public confidence and faith has been shattered.

It is an indictment against an impotent system that panders to the criminal with his rich endowment of rights and freedoms. This system, which so exhausts itself in the pursuit of the rights of the accused that its purpose is obscured and the victim is all but forsaken, is engendering an escalating enmity and contempt among the citizens who pay for it. Angry voices are starting to question the ineffectual tinkering of law reformers and are demanding a complete overhaul of the criminal justice system. Yesterday, those voices spoke with reverence for the rule of law and with pride in our concept of justice. Today, they are the voices of dissent, the angry voices of potential vigilantes.

Foreword

Not all lawyers love the law or even the practice of law. The practice, however, generates more than dusty legal text books and dry legal judgments. Beneath the burden of paper, there lie incredible stories. It is these stories, particularly when told by a master storyteller like Jack Montgomery, that bind us to our profession.

In this book, the author has turned his legal skills and literary sensitivity to an account of the murder of Ruby Adriaenssens. While the text addresses the senseless and brutal murder of a child by a young killer, it also points an accusatory finger at our legal system.

The James case is but further demonstrable evidence of the need for change so that the victim will be afforded a louder voice within the legal system.

Ruby's story is perpetuated in the Law Reports under the citation "R. v. J.T.J." The legacy of R. v. J.T.J. lives on in courtrooms across the country.

The Young Offenders Act continues to be a source of controversy. Daily, judges struggle with this act which governs both children who shoplift and teenagers who commit murder. Many cry out for its abolition; others, for drastic amendment. The process of change has begun, but it is far from complete.

Within the legal community, Mr. Montgomery is known as many things: a gentleman of the first rank, an extremely able lawyer and, at times, a rapscallion. No one who has seen "Hollywood Jack" in action could forget the unique blend of style, zeal, fairness and kindness he brings to the courtroom. "Montgomery for the prosecution" is always a promise of something special.

This, then, is the story of Ruby Adriaenssens as told by the man who prosecuted her murderer.

Cathy Everett, Department of Justice
Winnipeg, February 1998

CHAPTER 1

"All things bright and beautiful,
All creatures great and small,
All things wise and wonderful,
The Lord God made them all."
—Cecil Frances Alexander (1818-1895)

New Beginnings

The old Inglis Block squats on the south side of Notre Dame Avenue, a busy artery from which traffic flows out of the heart of the city's business and financial district, a mile to the east.

The shabby, three-storey, reddish-brown brick apartment building is afflicted with age and neglect. The oak staircases and doors and panels are deeply scored and marred. Yellowish-green, fly-specked paint chips drop from walls and ceilings.

The building sits on the northern flank of a district also in decay. After sundown, a nocturnal parade of drunks and night prowlers weaves and slithers past the block's dingy doorway. Once upon a time, this was a pleasant, safe neighbourhood. Hedges were clipped and grass was kept cut. Everyone grew flowers. Now the neighbourhood has gone to seed. Worse still, it is a jungle. No longer on warm summer evenings do old-timers rock on their verandahs. They lock themselves indoors and pray they will be safe.

Apartment 9 on the third floor of the crumbling Inglis Block was home to Kim Adriaenssens and her two children, Ruby and

Linda. Kim had been born in the little Manitoba town of Swan Lake on November 21, 1961. She had five sisters, two older and three younger. Her brother, Shane, arrived when she was five. Although she was bright, she disliked school and quit at the end of Grade 9.

Carmelo, a local baker, had taken a fancy to the pretty teenager and persuaded Kim to live with him. She was barely 17 when Linda was born. Three years later, on June 5, 1982, she had her second child, Ruby. Carmelo never abused the children, but the young mother could no longer withstand the beatings he gave her. The common-law relationship ended after six stormy years. Kim found herself alone with Linda and eight-month-old Ruby.

The lady from the agency had been blunt.

"Of course it would be better for you and the children in these circumstances," she said.

But Kim vowed that no one would take her children from her as long as there was a breath of life left in her body. She played with them, sang to them, read to them. She bathed and scrubbed them until they glowed. She prepared simple, nourishing meals for them. She lived for them, and she loved them with all her heart. The flighty, irresponsible high school dropout had, in a few short years, matured wondrously. Her daughters were her sacred trust, a trust she would never betray.

With nothing more than an abiding faith, Kim left Swan Lake with her family for new beginnings in the large, distant city to the south. She had courage, tenacity, boundless love and a strong instinct for survival. In Winnipeg she quickly discovered that there were warm hearts and many helpful hands extended.

Her mother Shirley, widowed after 23 contented years of marriage, lived just downstairs in Apartment 4 with two of Kim's siblings—Tania, 13, and Shane, 18. If Kim opened her door, walked down eight steps, did a 180-degree turn, and walked down eight more steps, she was at her mother's apartment in less than 30 seconds. Kim's Aunt Marlene and her two children also lived in the building. It was comforting to be surrounded by so many family members.

Kim accepted her first monthly welfare cheque which enabled her to carry on, but she longed for the day when she would become self-supporting.

The bulk of the money she received went to the landlord. Most of the remainder was spent on groceries. Kim was a cautious shopper and bargain-hunter. Her apartment was small, her furnishings sparse and tattered, though carefully tended. No new dresses hung in her closet.

Every extra nickel, dime and quarter went into a jar labelled "Treats" that sat on a shelf in Kim's kitchen. From this modest reservoir, she financed her one self-indulgence—bowling. Had there been surplus dollars in her purse, no doubt she would have been one of the faithful at the Saratoga Lanes on Donald Street, just off Notre Dame and a few short blocks from home. But the outings were few and far between. Young Linda was always at her mother's heels, even on those rare occasions when Kim could go to the bowling alley.

Friday, the 13th

It was shortly after 6 p.m. on a warm and lovely September day in 1985. Kim took a handful of coins from the "Treats" jar and dropped them into her change purse.

"Thanks, Mom, for coming up to babysit Ruby," she said as she bent down in the doorway and kissed her younger daughter. Ruby promised to be good and to listen to her grandmother.

Kim smiled at them happily as she closed the apartment door.

Linda clutched her mother's hand and practised her "giant steps" as they set off down Notre Dame Avenue for the Saratoga Lanes.

Just about the time that Kim and Linda had finished bowling their first game, Samay Suvannasorn was picking up his new car, a surprise for his wife, at a Nissan dealership across town. He drove the shiny, dark blue Sentra into the garage behind the white house with blue trim at 695 Sherbrook Street. It was very close to 8 p.m.

Samay was a short, handsome Laotian. His luminous and expressive eyes danced across the Sentra's gleaming surface in one final, glorious inspection. As he left the garage, he did not shut the overhead door that fronted onto the lane or the wooden door on the west wall. Samay had been working nights and was tired. He went straight to bed and slept undisturbed until morning.

The bread had to be out of the oven by 8 p.m. Shirley took Ruby down to Apartment 4, completed her domestic chores, then went back to Kim's suite.

Ruby stayed behind as her Aunt Tania and two companions began to watch a movie, *The Cannonball Run*, on television. After a few minutes, Ruby wanted to rejoin her grandmother. Tania opened the apartment door to let the three-year-old into the stairwell.

The reunion never happened. Somewhere on the 16 steps up to Apartment 9, the little one was snatched.

CHAPTER 2

"Tears are the silent language of grief."
—Voltaire (1694-1778)

Saturday, the 14th

Samay woke early, his new car on his mind. He went out to the garage with a piece of carpet that he was going to put inside the car to keep it from getting dirty. He stepped through the doorway on the west wall...and then he saw her.

He recoiled in horror. A little girl lay on her side in front of the Sentra. Dazed, yet drawn forward, he gazed, fighting nausea; then, suddenly, as if a fog had lifted, he saw the bloodied child clearly and he knew she was dead.

Whirling, his heart pounding, he ran to the house.

"In the garage at the rear of 695 Sherbrook," he stammered breathlessly.

The call was recorded at 8:25 a.m. The controlled voice of the dispatcher at the communications centre broadcast the location. The response was swift and loud. A fleet of racing ambulance, fire rescue and police vehicles converged on the murder scene.

Rescue Unit No. 2 cleared the fire station at Sargent and Burnell at 8:25 a.m. It spun off Cumberland and into the lane behind the garage just three minutes after Samay's frenzied call.

The ambulance wheeled into the lane at 8:29.

Constable Barry Steinthorson manoeuvred Cruiser Car 1101

between the ambulance and fire rescue wagon at 8:32. Within seconds, he and his partner, Constable Laverne Irvine, had taken up positions on the east and west sides of the garage to secure the site.

At 8:40 a.m., Sergeant Wayne Webb, the street supervisor, took charge of the uniformed personnel.

By 8:50, Detective Sergeants Morin and Shipman had arrived. Only 25 minutes had elapsed since the alarm.

The detectives were briefed by the uniformed officers, and then they moved quickly out of the huddle and over to the door on the west side of the garage. Their trained eyes swept the interior—darting, searching, now focusing on the body of the slain child: head to the south; feet to the north; face turned to the west; positioned on her front between a parked automobile— Nissan, licence number 966-CHL—and the west wall, in close proximity to the entrance door. The child was nude from the waist down; clothed only in a red and white T-shirt; lying on a pair of red overalls; head lying in a small pool of blood on its left side. A quantity of blood had trickled down the chin, indicating that at one time she was standing up and bleeding. Fecal staining was evident over the genital area and buttocks; there was similar staining on the back of the T-shirt. A concrete cinder block lay 2 1/2 to three feet southwest of the child's head.

Tough cops don't cry very often. But David Shipman cried that morning. So did Ronald Morin.

They stood in silence, heads bowed as if in prayer, their eyes transfixed upon the child's face. They looked down on her battered body, partly clad, the matted hair entangled in a spill of clotted blood. Neither spoke.

The grisly handiwork of the killer is commonplace on the robbery/homicide beat. Some cops who work it long enough get a little jaded. They do not weep over the corpses of those who have sealed their fate with their foul mouths and piggish greed. But this murder was different. It was the ultimate sacrilege, the defilement and destruction of something pure and sweet and sinless.

Both Morin and Shipman had long ago earned the respect of their brother officers inside the detective division and among members of the uniform branch as well. They arrested more than their fair share of killers and robbers, though some said (perhaps with a tinge of envy) that Shipman occasionally walked on the edge.

Clean-shaven, cherubic-faced, Shipman resembled an aging Vienna choir boy. Many of the females he collared fell in love with him. Now and again, he was bedevilled, in turn, by some lady's amorous advance. But there also were plenty of people who didn't take a shine to Big Dave on first meeting. In fact, most of the males Shipman busted hastily found good reason to hate his guts.

Morin was a bit of an enigma. He had the look of a white-haired leprechaun, but could still run faster than a greyhound. Despite his gregarious nature, he walked several solitary miles each day and never went to the Call Box Lounge where other cops unwound.

He had just cause to stay away. Long ago, he and two buddies went to Minneapolis to celebrate their high school graduation. Morin still hadn't figured out why it happened. The rashness of misguided youth perhaps? An excess of good American beer? But he joined the United States Marine Corps that weekend, and the brief holiday away from home became somewhat extended. He wound up in Vietnam.

Morin was no stranger to violent death. In the jungles of Southeast Asia, as in the jungles of his native city, he had looked at scores of mangled bodies with clinical objectivity. Now he knelt beside the body of a child. For the first time in his career, he fought back the tears. They flowed anyway. Slowly he got to his feet and squinted at his partner through misty eyes.

"The rotten bastard," he said to Shipman. "The dirty, rotten bastard."

Two very angry lawmen moved away from the broken body. They wouldn't sleep until the murderer was locked in his cell.

At 9:25 a.m., Sergeant Wayne Bellingham and his squad piled

out of the identification van lugging their cameras, cases and a vacuum cleaner.

After a fast briefing, Constable Craig Boan went to work with his camera, photographing the yard and garage. Constable Bruce Devries dusted for fingerprints, while Bellingham went down on his hands and knees beside the body to start the painstaking search for the hairs and fibres he knew he would find, the ones that would tie the killer to the crime.

"Why the hell do I stay in Ident.?" Bellingham asked rhetorically. "What the hell's the big fascination?"

He knew very well why he stayed. He believed that judges and juries could draw the proper inferences when presented with the right circumstantial evidence. An accused's confession, in contrast, all too easily could be tossed out of court.

"Thank God for good circumstantial evidence," the sergeant often told his colleagues. "There lies the real proof beyond all reasonable doubt. We just have to keep digging and digging. As far as I'm concerned, a confession is nothing more than icing on the cake."

Identification officers are highly trained and skilled forensic technicians. But there is much more to them than that. They are the searchers and collectors. They rifle society's garbage bins. They probe its laundry hampers for its dirty linen, its semen-stained shorts and blood-soaked jeans. They crawl on hands and knees in their community's dirt, its broken glass and its vomit to discover those elusive hairs and fibres embedded in the bloody filth. Perhaps the Sermon on the Mount[1] is part of their training doctrine—"Seek, and ye shall find." They usually do.

Bellingham and Devries had been at work in the garage for barely three minutes when the tall figure of Dr. Peter Markesteyn stepped through the side door at 9:30 a.m. Quietly, the officers exited through the rear. They would resume their hunt after the preliminary medical observations had been made.

Markesteyn paused as his eyes adjusted in the semi-darkness to the tableau of death at his feet. Hawk-like, he sighted the cinder block no more than three feet away from the child's face. His eyes then focused on the clump of hair adhering to the block's surface and on the blood-soaked, matted hair on top of the child's tiny head. He crouched by the body. While the fingers of his left hand traversed the pebbled concrete surface of the block, the sensitive fingers of his right hand gently pressed against the child's fragile skull, then grazed her bruised and pallid cheeks.

The doctor left the garage five minutes later. He asked one of the officers to arrange for the body to be transported to Children's Hospital as soon as the identification team had finished its work. Another 10 minutes and Markesteyn was in the pathology department preparing for the post-mortem examination.

Devries carefully placed clear plastic tape onto the child's legs and lower body. Slowly he removed the tape and mounted it on plastic backing. Any hairs and fibres clinging to the skin were now preserved for microscopic examination. He took a new brown paper bag from the identification vehicle and placed it over the upper body. Then, after wrapping the child in a new plastic shroud, he and Constable Peter Luczenczyn conveyed the body to the hospital.

Boan had photographed the victim from every conceivable angle and had filmed the garage inside and out. He left for the Inglis Block, anxious to get some shots of the stairwell between the second and third floors. Bellingham, meanwhile, still crawled around the garage floor, peering at the dusty rubble.

A grim-faced young officer delivered the news to Kim Adriaenssens.

"We've found Ruby," he told her. His strong hands gripped her forearms. He spoke tenderly. "She's dead."

On that awful Saturday morning, Shirley told her children that Ruby's body had been found. Tania wept against her mother's breast, but Shane's face flushed with anger. The revelation numbed him. He struggled to visualize the killer.

At 4:02 p.m., Shane, in company with Constable Lyle Rance and Detective James Townsend, walked into the morgue area on the fourth floor of Children's Hospital. Markesteyn was waiting for them.

Shane had volunteered to identify his niece. He stood at the end of the examining table, staring at Ruby's lifeless form.

"Why did this have to happen to her? She was so good. She never hurt anyone," he said, lips quivering. He then squared his shoulders and turned away.

"You've got to find the killer," he told Rance as they retraced their steps along the antiseptic corridor. "Somebody's got to pay for this."

CHAPTER 3

The Search for a Killer

Throughout the day of September 14, a small army of police officers, 67 strong, combed miles of back alleys. They searched apartment building basements, sheds and garages. Dozens of boxes and bags and countless pails and hampers were upended in musty closets and cluttered cellars. A thousand dirty garments tumbled out, all to be examined for blood and seminal staining. One team of detectives checked the roster of active pedophiles, ferreted them out and interrogated them.

One hundred and eighty-six people were questioned. Some were suspects, others potential witnesses. Some, it was hoped, would offer useful information.

Among those interviewed by Sergeant Darryl Preisentanz and Constable Derek Gove were Betty Lynn Gouvreau, 12, and her little sister Rachel. They lived in the Inglis Block with their mother Debbie.

Betty Lynn told them that her mom's cousin, John James Jr., and a friend had come to her suite between 5:30 p.m. and 6 p.m. Friday while her mother was at bingo. John asked to go the bathroom and stayed for no more than five or 10 minutes.

At 7:16 p.m., Preisentanz and Gove ushered John James Jr. into Interview Room No. 1 in the detective division on the second floor of the Public Safety Building. The trio sat down at a small table.

James was no more suspect than Betty Lynn Gouvreau. He

was just one among many to be questioned during the course of the investigation. Neither Preisentanz nor Gove had even been aware of his existence one hour earlier.

The mood was relaxed. James was interviewed in routine fashion, beginning at 7:16 p.m., then again at 7:49 p.m. The questions put and the answers given were recorded in the officers' notebooks. This was the fixed order of doing things. Routine questions. Questions and answers all written down. Standard police work. Just more information to be typed into a supplementary occurrence report at the end of an extra-long shift.

Another routine question. An answer that brought both officers to full alert.

"I can't rat, man. I wasn't there, but I know what you're talking about. What are you going to do if I get wiped out by his brother, man?"

"We are talking about a dead three-year-old girl, John," the sergeant said tersely.

"I don't know if you'll catch him. He's heading out today."

"Who?"

"Eli Tacan. He's from Sioux Valley."

"What about Eli Tacan?"

"He said he'd seen a little girl. I don't believe him because he was drunk. He said he took her into this garage a half a block or two away. He said he got fucking scared, man."

"Then what?"

"He said, 'The fucking pigs won't get me for this. I'll be long gone.'"

"Did he say where?"

"Sioux Valley, I think. He's from there."

"Where's Sioux Valley?"

"Twenty minutes from Brandon."

"Why did he take the girl to the garage?"

"He was charged with it before in Sioux Valley. He said he was catching a bus this morning or tomorrow, I don't remember."

A suspect had surfaced.

Preisentanz asked James to wait in the interview room. While Gove apprised other officers of James's revelation, Preisentanz did a fast check on the Canadian Police Information Centre computer system. Eli Tacan's name was there.

The officers returned to the room at 9 p.m.

"How old is Eli?" the sergeant asked.

"Twenty-three, maybe a few years older," James replied.

"Who is his brother you referred to?"

"David."

"Can you tell us again what Eli said to you?"

"Yeah, like I said, he came back and said he saw the little girl on the stairs. He took her to a garage and she was crying for her grandmother."

"Then what did he say?"

"He said he wouldn't get caught and that—and then started laughing and telling jokes."

Gove asked James to repeat everything slowly so that it could be written down. James obliged and signed the statement.

Again, they left him in the interview room. Approximately 12 hours had elapsed since the body of the murdered child was found.

The Confession

Usually on a Saturday night around 11 o'clock, the large area that houses the detective division is relatively quiet. That night, however, it was a latter-day Bedlam.

Well-groomed detectives collaborated with their grubby counterparts, the ones in the sweaty T-shirts and jeans who had been working the "tenderloin." Uniformed men and women rushed in with pink copies of occurrence reports. Messages were recorded and delivered. In 12 short hours, the small army had generated surprisingly large piles of paper. At every desk, heavy shoulders hunched over ancient Underwoods, while sausage fingers beat out noisy, two-fingered tattoos. Telephones rang incessantly and competed with the clacking keys. A steady stream of citizens occupied the interview rooms that bordered the space. The noise level rose in direct proportion to the increased flow of traffic. It would take an exceptionally well-adjusted man to hear himself think in this madhouse.

One such man sat at his desk in a far corner of the command post, totally oblivious to the racket round about. Sergeant Angus Anderson had come on duty at 4 p.m. After a cursory briefing, he began to absorb the contents of the growing pile of reports and statements. He digested every detail.

Anderson's soft voice and warm smile belied his toughness. He had the appearance and demeanour of one who had taken holy orders. He was known among Crown counsel as "the Reverend Angus."

His young partner, Detective Cal Osborne, had been his understudy since transferring from the uniform branch to robbery/homicide. Anderson persistently called him by his baptismal name, Calvin, slyly relishing its ecclesiastical overtones. Osborne had to live with it.

It was 10:23 p.m. Anderson was concentrating on a statement that Derek Gove had handed to him moments before. He riffled through a sheaf of papers, then extracted and quickly scanned statements that had been obtained from Corrine Marie Demas and Ferlon James Goosehead. What they had said didn't square at all with what James had told Gove and Preisentanz. There were just too many discrepancies and inconsistencies.

Anderson beckoned to his partner, who was banging on a typewriter three desks away. Osborne came over and stood behind, trying in vain to read James's statement as Anderson kept spearing it with his right index finger.

"This guy is jerking us around, Calvin," Anderson said softly. "Let's go find out why."

James was still seated at the table in the interview room. Anderson introduced himself and his partner, then said they were investigating the murder of a three-year-old girl on Friday night. He referred to what James and his friend Goosehead had told police.

"It appears to us that you're lying to us about your knowledge of what happened last night. You've got to know more about what happened last night than you're telling us. Why don't you tell us what really happened?"

James stared at the floor for about 10 seconds, then said, "I barely remember."

"Do you remember anything at all about the little girl?" Anderson asked.

"Yeah," James said. "I grabbed her. I took her to a garage down the lane. I can't remember that well. I blacked out."

Anderson tried to anticipate the inevitable judicial roadblocks that lay ahead. He had learned long ago that there were times when a police officer needed more than Job's patience and Solomon's wisdom. He also was required to have an encyclopedic knowledge of the criminal law and the capacity to apply its many nuances with all the dexterity of a Philadelphia lawyer. Otherwise, he would not escape the ire of some of the stuffier, more pedantic judges.

The sergeant knew James was 17 years old. The police would have to comply strictly with the provisions of the Young Offenders Act if James's confession to the murder was ever to be considered by a jury. They must make it very clear to him that he had the right to consult with counsel, or a parent, or, in the absence of a parent, an adult relative.

Anderson also knew that one of John's relatives, Harry James, was among the many citizens police had brought into the Public Safety Building for interviews. John had identified Harry as his uncle.

The sergeant raised his right hand. "Hold on a minute. I'll get your uncle. Do you want your uncle here?"

"Yeah," James replied.

At 11:07 p.m., Anderson and Osborne left James in the room and went directly to the juvenile division where they located Harry James. While walking back, Harry told them he was John's second cousin, not his uncle.

After the men re-entered the room, Anderson turned to John James Jr. and said, "I am arresting you for the murder, on the 13th of September, 1985, of Ruby Adriaenssens, three years of age, of Suite 9, 628 1/2 Notre Dame Avenue, Winnipeg. It is my duty to inform you that you have the right to retain and instruct counsel without delay. Do you understand?"

"Yeah," James answered. "I want to get in touch with my lawyer."

"You are not bound to say anything, but anything you do say will be taken down in writing and may be used as evidence. Do you understand?"

"Yeah," muttered James.

"Who do you want to call?"

James reached into the pocket of his sweatpants and pulled out his lawyer's card. Osborne took him to a quiet, unoccupied office nearby. The detective dialled Brenda Keyser's home telephone number, let it ring, handed the phone to James and then left, closing the door behind him. The lawyer and her client spoke privately for the next three minutes.

At 11:52, James was escorted back to the interview room.

"We've got to take your clothes, John," Anderson said as he handed over a pair of blue pants, a blue top and blue slippers.

James started to remove his T-shirt, then looked at Anderson and asked, "When will I get them back?"

"Probably you won't."

Off came the black, short-sleeved T-shirt and the black Thunderbird sweatpants with a wide yellow stripe down one leg. Off came the Power running shoes. Off came the purple undershorts and soiled white socks.

Anderson and Osborne tagged and bagged the items in plastic, while James pulled on the substitutes. After the detectives parcelled and initialled the prisoner's old black leather jacket and black Dutch Boy peaked cap, Anderson asked James for hair samples.

Some small insects fell onto a piece of white bond paper as James combed his hair. Anderson folded the paper over into a pharmacist's envelope and placed it in a plastic bag. He had James pull some hairs and drop them onto another piece of white paper which also was folded into an envelope and placed in a bag. He then asked James to comb his pubic hair, cut some pubic hair with a small pair of scissors, and pluck some pubic hairs onto another piece of paper. Finally, he helped James scrape his fingernails onto paper; then he went to find some nail clippers.

Lawyer Brenda Keyser was waiting at the front counter. Anderson told her they were in the midst of seizing physical evidence and returned to the interview room. James clipped the nails from his right and left hands onto separate pieces of paper. He was co-operative throughout.

Osborne escorted James to the washroom at 12:20 a.m. The detectives then met with Keyser in the staff inspector's office to brief her on the details of the offence.

At 12:32 a.m., the lawyer attended in the interview room alone with her client. She came out about one minute later to request a cigarette for him.

At 1:09 a.m., she again came out and asked to speak to Harry James, who was in the interview room next door. She stayed until 1:24 a.m. She had spent 37 minutes with John and 15 minutes with Harry James.

The officers took the younger James to the identification office for photographing and fingerprinting. They were back in the interview room by 1:45 a.m.

James declined something to eat, but agreed to a cup of coffee. By 1:50 a.m., Osborne had returned with both coffee and cigarettes. Between puffs and sips, James filled the officers in on his background. Osborne dutifully wrote in his notebook, while Anderson sat back and studied their prisoner.

Five feet, nine inches tall; 135 pounds; skinny build; black hair, over the collar, wavy, combed back, no part; no facial hair; oval face; slightly pointed chin; brown eyes; small scar on right eyebrow; nose flattened and broken—he had allowed nature to heal it; small scar on centre finger of right hand between nail and first joint; heart with a ribbon tattooed on right biceps; cross on right forearm; initials "J.R." on left forearm.

His full name was John Thomas James Jr. He was born on August 31, 1968 in Winnipeg and raised mostly in foster homes. He attended school in Brandon, Manitoba; and had a Grade 10 education. His mother died in 1975. He had lived at 89 Lorne Avenue, Winnipeg, for the past 3 1/2 months with Harry James.

John was single, but had been in a common-law relationship with Barbara Atkinson, 17, of the Roseau River Indian Reserve. They had been separated for four months after living together for 10. James contended that he supported their four-month-old baby, Naomi Christine Fay, when he could.

He was employed by Harry in private roofing around the city. His father, John James Sr., lived on the Roseau River Reserve and also worked as a roofer.

The younger James had no social insurance number and no driver's licence. It was also noted that he had no cash on his person. However, he did carry a copy of a probation order which Judge Phillip Ashdown had signed at Emerson just 3 1/2 weeks earlier. James had been placed on a year's probation after entering guilty pleas on three charges of break and entry.

It was while he was bound over to keep the peace and be of good behaviour that he had slain his tiny victim.

The Confession Continued

Osborne put his pen down and rubbed his eyes. There was a quiet dignity about him. No matter how tired or pressured or angered he was, in his 10 years on the force he had always played by the Queensberry Rules. He addressed John quietly.

"You've had the opportunity to speak to a lawyer. Do you want to make a written statement about what happened last night?"

"No. She told me not to."

"We've spoken to Goosehead as well as to others in the area and we've read the statement that you gave to the other officers about where you were when this thing happened. It's obvious to us that you lied to us. We know that you were at the Maryland Hotel with Ferlon Goosehead and Corrine Demas at about eight o'clock on the 13th of September. We also know that you were making advances toward Corrine and it appears to us that she rejected your advances. You were trying to pick up Corrine on Friday night, weren't you?"

"No," James replied.

"The people we have spoken to say they saw Corrine and a male kissing in the corridor of the Inglis Block. Goosehead said it wasn't him, so I would think it was you trying to pick her up."

"Yeah, okay."

"We know you left the hotel. Where did you go?"

"The same place where Corrine was—Debbie's place."

"Debbie's place?"

Now Osborne knew that James had returned to the Inglis Block where Ruby lived. Hours before, Osborne had read Corrine Demas's written statement. Neither fatigue nor the passage of time had yet affected his rather remarkable capacity for total recall.

Corrine had said: "I went up to Suite 8. That's Debbie's suite. When I got there she wasn't there, but her two daughters were—Rachel and Betty Lynn."

Osborne spoke softly, almost in a whisper. "You were at Debbie's block?"

"Yeah. I saw her walking up the stairs."

"What made you grab her?"

James didn't reply. He just sat, staring down at the floor, his head shaking from side to side. Apart from the sounds of his erratic breathing, it was deathly quiet in the room.

The race against time was over. Softly, patiently, almost sadly, Osborne spoke to James again.

"Did you carry her from the block?"

James raised his eyes slowly and looked at Osborne, then at Anderson. At last he answered.

"No, she walked."

"Did you hold her?"

"Yeah, I held her hand."

"Did you know her?"

"I never seen her before."

"Where did you go?"

"To the garage."

"Was she scared?"

"Yeah. She was screaming loud. She was calling for her grandmother."

"Then what did you do?"

"I blacked out."

Osborne is no different from police officers everywhere. He, too, is a father. He strained hard to suppress his own emotions and the recurring visions of his own youngster who was barely older than Ruby. He rubbed his eyes again and fixed his gaze upon the prisoner.

"John, it's a very tragic thing that happened. For everyone. It's probably hard for you to talk about it. But I think you remember what happened."

James was becoming visibly distressed. He began to shake.

"Did you get scared?"

"Yeah."

"You removed her pants and panties?"

James made no reply. He raised his right hand from his lap and held it against his right eyebrow. He was becoming more agitated.

"Did you enter her?"

Again he made no verbal reply, but he nodded in the affirmative.

"Did you enter her vagina?"

Another affirmative nod as James said, "I tried."

Osborne pressed for further details of the sexual assault. He established that the accused had tried to enter the child's rectum, that he hadn't ejaculated, that the child was crying and screaming.

"Did you have to kill her?" the detective asked, his voice barely above a whisper.

James hesitated. His eyes started to water. He was again shaking and trembling.

"I heard someone in the lane. She wouldn't be quiet."

"Did you throw her down?"

Again James hesitated before answering. Tears started rolling down his cheeks.

"I hit her."

"With what?"

"A brick."

"How many times?"

James had removed his right hand from his eyebrow. Now he lifted it slightly off the table and held up his middle and index fingers, indicating twice. The hand was trembling almost uncontrollably.

"John, I know you can talk. Can you tell me how many times you hit her?"

Again James raised his trembling hand from the table and extended two fingers.

"Then what happened?"

"I left."

Osborne seemed lost in thought. Finally he said to James, "Did you know you killed her?"

"I thought so," was the reply.

While it is improbable that John James accepted, as an article of his faith, that confession is good for the soul, it nevertheless seemed to be good for his body. Almost immediately, the shaking and trembling stopped. He appeared to relax.

Osborne then asked, "Do you want to tell us about it in a written statement?"

James paused. "Let me think about it."

"Okay. We'll give you a few minutes."

Osborne and Anderson left the room. On their return eight minutes later, they found James was not willing to give his statement in writing.

At 3:40 a.m., Anderson drove a police car up the ramp from the garage beneath the Public Safety Building. Osborne sat directly behind the sergeant. James, his hands cuffed behind his back, sat on Osborne's right. They were en route to the Manitoba Youth Centre in the city's west end.

Almost as an afterthought, Anderson changed course and swung west onto Notre Dame. Seven minutes later, he stopped in front of the Inglis Block. He turned to look at James.

"Is this where Debbie's place is?"

"Yeah."

"What door did you come out of with the little girl?"

James looked directly at the front door.

"That one there."

"Will you show us where you took the girl?"

"Yeah."

The trio got out of the car. James led the officers south down the east side of the Inglis Block, across an empty parking lot and straight down a lane.

"Was there anybody around?" Anderson asked.

"Yeah. There was three people in the lane."

At a point where the lane intersects with Cumberland Avenue, James stopped abruptly, stiffened, started to shake again and said, "That's far enough."

"Well, this isn't where it happened, is it?" the sergeant asked.

"No, it's across the street."

They crossed Cumberland and went down the lane to the garage behind 695 Sherbrook Street.

"Did you go through the big door?"

"No, the little door on the other side."

James led the officers to the west side of the garage.

"Is this where it happened?" Anderson asked as he pointed to an area in front of Samay Suvannasorn's new car.

"Yeah."

"Where did you get the brick from?" Anderson moved toward the south wall. "Over here?"

James swung his arms to the right side of his body and gestured toward the west wall. "No, right here, against this wall."

As the three returned to the police car, Anderson continued to probe.

"Did you walk down the lane when you left?"

"No," James replied. "I came back onto the street."

"Then where did you go?"

"To the 7-Eleven."

"Which one?"

"On Spence."

"What did you do then?"

"Bought a Big Gulp and went home."

It was 4:06 a.m. when John Thomas James Jr. was delivered into the hands of youth centre personnel.

CHAPTER 4

Mopping Up

The identification section was housed unsatisfactorily in cramped quarters at the south end of the detective division. It was here, behind a desk in the middle of a row, that Craig Boan laboured. He had never known the luxury of total absorption in one case at a time. There were always several on the go contemporaneously.

Boan was the designated exhibits officer in the Adriaenssens case. By Sunday afternoon, the 15th, his desk had started to become the repository for all the physical evidence gathered during the investigation.

The first lot to arrive was unloaded by Bruce Devries—a substantial conglomeration of vials, tubes and swabs containing bodily secretions, liver, kidney and dried blood samples, hairs and fibres, all removed from or near Ruby's body.

The next afternoon, as Boan worked on a scale drawing of another murder scene, he glimpsed Angus Anderson smiling at him sheepishly.

"You're doing the Lord's work, son," the "Reverend Angus" confided while stacking vials of fingernail scrapings, head hair and pubic hair, all neatly labelled, on the last remnant of unoccupied desk space.

Boan grinned. He, like Anderson, was a contented police officer. Tall (six feet, seven inches), bespectacled, considerate and soft-spoken, he was not dissimilar in many ways to Clark Kent. Although his choice of professional activity now kept him off the streets, he still jogged and pumped a little iron, "just in case."

Anderson returned to the identification section twice that afternoon laden with boxes of shoes and clothing seized from the person and residence of the killer. Each time the sergeant appeared, Boan stood and thanked him for having personally delivered the exhibits—and he again acknowledged, as he must since Anderson outranked him, that he was indeed doing the Lord's work.

No sooner had the sergeant departed for the last time than Wayne Bellingham and Peter Luczenczyn carted in a 50-pound cinder block. They placed it, along with seven pieces of concrete, in front of Boan's desk. The block and crumbling masonry had been found slightly west of the deceased child's head. On a return visit to the cluttered compound, the officers brought the clothing the child had been wearing, now catalogued and wrapped in plastic.

Again the young leviathan rose and thanked his associates for their valued contributions. He eyed the depressing pile of material on the floor beside him. There are those who might well have suggested less conspicuous places where the exhibits could have been shoved.

At sunrise on Tuesday, the 17th, Bellingham returned to the garage for a final search through the dust and debris. By 9:30 a.m., he was back in the identification section, collaborating with his fellow collectors, Boan and Devries. The officers were confident that, among the 71 items taken from the crime scene, the body of the deceased and the body of the accused, they would find vitally significant circumstantial evidence for a jury's consideration.

During the tedious selection process, they sifted and sorted and conferenced, then selected or rejected. Among the few things seized that would escape microscopic scrutiny by the crime lab scientists was a Kentucky Fried Chicken carton retrieved from under the Sentra. No prints had been lifted from its greasy surface, so it was tossed into Boan's wastebasket.

Bellingham patiently picked through the grimy contents of the vacuum bag with a pair of tweezers. Eventually, he withdrew what appeared to be a pubic hair. He rummaged through the items that Anderson had delivered and found the vial containing John James's plucked pubic hair.

Positioned in front of a window, he held the tweezers, still clamping the pubic hair, up to the light. He squinted into the vial. Gradually, a look of intense satisfaction crossed his tanned face.

Bellingham was always searching for what he termed "the right circumstantial evidence." He was a little more than cautiously optimistic that forensic scientists would confirm the evidential importance of his most recent discovery.

He walked toward his partners, smiling knowingly. Somewhat indelicately perhaps, he shared with them his own evaluation of the find.

"Fellas, I think we've got John Thomas James Jr. by the short hairs."

By 11:30 a.m., the potential exhibits had been loaded into a police van which Boan piloted across town to the R.C.M.P. Crime Detection Laboratory. There, he tracked down James Ernest Cadieux, a recognized expert in hair and fibre analysis.

The giant Boan greeted the brilliant, diminutive scientist with warmth and enthusiasm. To the casual observer, the awesome contrast in the men's stature must have evoked visions of the mythical David and Goliath.

Boan knew that Cadieux would hastily turn his talents toward microscopic confirmation of the "Bellingham boast"—that police indeed had the accused by the short hairs.

The murder investigation, which had begun just four days earlier, was virtually complete. It had never lost momentum.

The police had performed with admirable dispatch. Dedication, teamwork, perseverance, sweat, a little bit of luck and then the inevitable arrest. But, as always, few bouquets; this, despite the fact the police had the killer some 14 1/2 hours after information was received concerning the slain child.

It was now the justice system's turn.

True to sluggish form, another 72 days would elapse before John Thomas James Jr. made his first appearance on a transfer hearing before Judge Edwin Kimelman.

CHAPTER 5

The Transfer

John James Jr. was 17 when he sodomized and killed Ruby Adriaenssens. He was a "young person" as defined in the Young Offenders Act; that is, he was over 12 and under 18 and, as such, subject to the jurisdiction of the youth court in the first instance.

If he was tried and found guilty in that forum, his maximum sentence would be three years in a place of detention for juvenile offenders. If, however, he was tried in adult court and found guilty, there was the theoretical possibility he would spend the rest of his life behind bars.

The Young Offenders Act provides a young person who has attained the age of 14 years, and is alleged to have committed an indictable offence (as, for example, murder), may on the order of a youth court be proceeded against in accordance with the law ordinarily applicable to an adult charged with the offence.

The very thought of transfer raises the stress level of some youth court judges. A transfer subjects the youth, they say, to the "harsh realities of Canada's criminal justice system."

"What harsh realities?" scores of police officers assigned to youth squads around the country would like to know.

"What harsh realities?" echo the prosecutors doing time in youth courts and the disillusioned custodial officers in charge of youth who find themselves in trouble with the law.

The Crown attorneys involved in the Adriaenssens case knew from past experience that James's transfer to adult court was anything but a certainty. They had witnessed some youth court judges clinging to the Declaration of Principle in the Young Offenders Act (see Appendix 1) with the evangelical fervour of the fundamentalist who literally interprets every word in Holy Writ.

The declaration's third tenet recognizes that young persons who commit offences require supervision, discipline and control, but, because of their state of dependency and level of development and maturity, they have special needs and require guidance and assistance.

A skilful application of this tenet by a timorous judge, or by one who labours under a sincere but myopic naïveté, could almost ensure that even a juvenile Jack the Ripper would never have to face a judge and jury.

Thursday, November 28, 1985

Elizabeth Sellick, the senior Crown attorney in charge of youth court prosecutors, assigned herself to the transfer hearing. She was determined that James would be tried in adult court.

She sat rigidly at the counsel table reviewing her notes, her expression tense. The clerk called for order and Associate Chief Judge Edwin C. Kimelman, a tall, distinguished-looking man, appeared.

It was as if a warm summer breeze had wafted across Sellick's face, gently blowing away her anxiety. She punctuated her robust "Good morning, your honour" with a cheerful smile.

She seemed to sense that Kimelman, unlike some of his youth court judicial brethren, could not quite subscribe to the philosophy that there really was no such thing as a bad boy.

The Crown's first witness, John James Sr., was called simply to attest to his son's age. He entered the witness box in an obstreperous mood, first refusing to be sworn in, then later balking at what he considered to be Sellick's "dumb questions." His anticipated testimony required all of 10 seconds at best.

Instead, several minutes passed before sufficient confirmation was obtained to enable Kimelman to rule that John James Jr. indeed was born on August 31, 1968.

Later, in his written reasons for judgment, Kimelman commented on the testimony of the father, observing that "the transcript of evidence fails to disclose his surly, belligerent and inappropriate attitude in court, his refusal to appropriately answer questions put to him by the Crown, and, more importantly, his attempt to apparently strike his son as he moved past him in the courtroom."

As the hearing progressed, Sellick produced a report setting out some of John James's activities since 1981—pursuits that could hardly qualify him as a misguided youth. He had been involved in serious criminal conduct for several years and had 32 prior offences:

1. February 19, 1981 .... theft under $200
2. February 20 .... forgery
3. February 20 .... uttering
4. March 9 .... theft over $200
5. March 10 .... break, enter and theft
6. March 10 .... break, enter and theft
7. March 10 .... theft over $200
8. March 11 .... mischief
9. March 11 .... theft under $200
10. March 12 .... break, enter and theft
11. March 12 .... break, enter with intent
12. March 13 .... assault causing bodily harm
13. March 13 .... break, enter and theft
14. March 16 .... robbery
15. April 2 .... robbery
16. April 3 .... robbery
17. April 10 .... break, enter with intent
18. April 15 .... break, enter and theft
19. May 11 .... wilful damage
20. May 15 .... break, enter with intent
21. July 18, 1982 .... break and enter

Kimelman listened attentively as the assistant superintendent of the Agassiz Youth Centre described the facility and its programs.

"How is security maintained?" Sellick asked.

A slight frown flickered across the judge's otherwise impassive face as he attempted to digest the answer.

"Security is maintained by the residents themselves, the peer groups," the official responded.

The court also heard from a correctional services officer who outlined the programs, mental health resources, levels of supervision, and provisions for release and social reintegration available at or through federal institutions in the justice system. The attentive judge wrote in his trial book continuously.

A psychologist testified on behalf of the defence. The balance of the hearing was consumed with counsels' submissions, Sellick pressing for trial in adult court, Brenda Keyser, James's lawyer, urging a hearing in the youth forum.

The ever-gracious Kimelman thanked counsel and reserved judgment.

Thursday, December 19

Kimelman's written decision was lengthy. He stated, in part:

"Defence counsel called Dr. Eric Ellis, an eminent child psychologist, whose credentials are well known to the court. Dr. Ellis had occasion to see the accused for one period of two hours and also read the available reports. Of unusual interest was the fact that, while Dr. Ellis was aware of the charge against the youth, he was not made aware of the circumstances of the offence. Whether this would have affected his testimony is pure conjecture and I choose not to speculate. He described the youth as having poor coping mechanisms, and being 'the most poorly adjusted to the circumstances of the situation.'

"The doctor went on to state that the youth required a structured environment and suggested a custodial disposition of between one and three years."

Kimelman carefully reviewed the evidence. He also reviewed the law as it relates to the transfer provisions in the Young Offenders Act. He noted, among other things:

"We are faced here, quite clearly, with a young person of violent nature who is a clear threat to the safety of society. Is this in itself sufficient reason for a transfer to the adult system?

"The offence, as previously stated, is one of the most serious in nature in the Criminal Code of Canada. It was perpetrated against a helpless, defenceless three-year-old child whose death was caused in a violent, brutal manner. While the accused had been drinking, the Crown alleges he was not drunk at the time. There is no rationale for the offence. The accused will be 18 in eight months; to all intents and purposes he is an adult in action and life-style. His background indicates a life of deprivation and abuse that may or may not have contributed to his almost perennial appearance in court. His prior record would appear to indicate his total disregard for the law. He has had probation involvement and the child welfare authorities had placed him in 11 group homes or foster homes since age four. He has resided in a specialized native treatment facility for a year. With this background of resource involvement he is back before the court, but this time for the offence of murder. It is of more than passing interest to note that he is the father of a five-month-old child, and he has not established any relationship with the child or mother since birth. The pattern seems to be recurring again.

"With this background of involvement, defence counsel suggests that her client can yet be rehabilitated within the resources available in the young offenders system. While Dr. Ellis…also appears to make this recommendation, he is not as unwavering as defence counsel, and…he makes his recommendation based only on one two-hour interview with the accused, and not knowing the facts surrounding the alleged offence.

"I must, with respect, disagree with the learned doctor."

The judge concluded his reasoned decision as follows: "Incarceration would appear to be the answer to the needs of this young person. It will act to prevent his criminal reinvolvement; he will receive some of the professional treatment available in the adult and federal institutions.

"I do not want my comments to be construed as deprecating the efforts and programs at Agassiz. I merely state that for this accused they are totally inadequate.

"I make this further observation. Courts should be reluctant to say that young persons will receive the type of treatment they need in the youth system without knowing something of the services, treatment and programs available. I have no evidence before me that the Agassiz programs, run by the accused's peers, supervised by lay staff, with leaves into the community on recommendation by those peers, are equal to or comparable to programs run in the federal institutions where, as the evidence indicated, professionals (psychologists and psychiatrists) are available. Contrary to what counsel states, the federal adult institutions would appear to offer some of the direct, professional input that this youth obviously needs.

"Finally, this court cannot overlook the fact that the youth court is restricted to a maximum three-year disposition against a youth, and even that term can be shortened if the provincial director moves him to an adult facility at age 18. In effect, we might be looking at a maximum of eight months in the youth system.

"The interests of society, having regard to the needs of the accused, require that he be proceeded against by indictment in the ordinary court, and I so order."

Chapter 6

"Do as adversaries do in law,
Strive mightily, but eat and drink as friends."
—Shakespeare, *The Taming of the Shrew*
(Act II, Scene 2)

The Preliminary Hearing

Judge Kimelman had removed James from the jurisdiction of the youth court. The next step in the snail-paced proceedings was the preliminary hearing, simply an inquiry before a provincial judge who would determine whether there was sufficient evidence to commit the accused to stand trial before judge and jury.

The hearing was scheduled to get under way before Judge Arnold Conner on Monday, March 3, 1986.

The citizens whose tax dollars pay for the administration of criminal justice might well ask why it would take 171 days from the time little Ruby's body was discovered until the sufficiency of the evidence against her accused killer was tested in a lower court.

Unlike many murder cases, this one was straightforward. The murderer had confessed. He told the police when, where and by what means he had killed his victim. He went even further and told them why. He was snared in a trap of deadly circumstantial evidence as well.

The bleary-eyed prosecutors—myself and Les Kee, assisted

by Kenneth Tacium—had dissected and ingested the contents of an awesome pile of paper generated by 67 policemen, two pathologists and three scientists.

We had further distorted our vision both physically and mentally as, night after night, we squinted over the reported judicial decisions concerning the admissibility of confessions by youthful troublemakers.

We had stalked the corridors of the Inglis Block and paced the back alleys near the Maryland Hotel and 695 Sherbrook Street. The area around the murder scene became as familiar to us as our own neighbourhoods. We even got to know some of the potential witnesses better than many of our own neighbours.

We were confident the case was a strong one.

John James Jr. snatched Ruby Adriaenssens on the evening of September 13, 1985, and then proceeded to destroy her.

A little child hopelessly imprisoned; defenceless; sodomized and brutalized; petrified beyond human understanding.

She was too small for James to enter vaginally, so he tried to penetrate her body from behind. She shrieked in pain and terror as he tore her anal ring.

He heard people in the lane. Ruby's screams would alert them. He smashed her head against a heavy cinder block. The blow broke her neck. Blood gushed from her right ear and ran down her chin. Her heart stopped beating.

We were confident, but not complacent. The outcome of a criminal trial is as unpredictable as a horse race.

There was another matter for our attention—the selection of photographs from the scores taken at the murder scene and post-mortem examination of the deceased child. Several copies would be required for court.

If there is anything at all to the old cliché that a picture is worth a thousand words, then some of Craig Boan's photographs were going to speak volumes.

Defence counsel usually fight hard to keep such pictures from the jurors' eyes. They always advance the same old argument in favour of suppression: The prejudicial effect will far outweigh any probative value the visual aids might have.

"The Crown is attempting to tender these photographs solely for the purpose of inflaming the passions of the jury," they whine.

This is not the case at all. Jurors seldom, if ever, are permitted to attend a crime scene. Photographs become a necessary and realistic substitute for the personal visitation. If a photograph of a victim, gruesome in death, was admitted in evidence and did in fact inflame a juror and prejudice his mind against the killer, then so be it. It would be the machinations of the killer, not those of the prosecutor, that inflamed and angered.

In mid-February, Boan met with us to begin the selection process. On a long table he laid out row upon row of pictures taken at the scene.

Another homicide. Another meeting. Selection and rejection. All routine work in trial preparation. A booklet of photographs would be produced and tendered in evidence. The jurors would virtually see the scene of the crime.

And they would see the child. And they would remember her as long as they lived.

She is nude from the waist down. Her head lies in a small pool of blood on the garage floor.

Her little face, in death, is serene and sweet and lovely. It reflects none of the pain, terror and torture she suffered just before the killer broke her neck.

Later on, when jurors did see that picture, many wept.

About a week before the preliminary inquiry was to start, Brenda Keyser made an appointment to see the Crown counsel who would prosecute her client.

It is customary before a major criminal trial for opposing counsel to discuss the case. Sometimes they agree upon certain facts, which dispenses with proof at trial and saves valuable court time. Essentially, the defence is given full and detailed particulars so there will be no surprises at trial.

Keyser was provided with copies of her client's statements and given an overview of the anticipated testimony of prospective witnesses.

The meeting ended and she rose to leave the office. She paused and leaned against a wall. Her eyes shifted from one Crown attorney to the other.

"Well, gentlemen, I can tell you this. If it had been my kid, there wouldn't even be a trial."

But it wasn't her kid.

And then she was gone.

The minutes ticked by. Neither prosecutor spoke. Never before had we heard such a remark pass a lawyer's lips. Before— or since.

There is a camaraderie among members of the bar. Naturally, in the heat of courtroom battles, tempers flare. But they cool, and warm friendships develop among the gladiators and are sustained down through the years. At the end of a trial, the opponents usually have a drink together.

But the battle lines were drawn on that cold, late February afternoon.

These adversaries would strive mightily, but they would never eat and drink as friends.

Monday, March 3, 1986

Court was called to order on the stroke of 10 o'clock—a good omen in that punctuality is not a high priority among some provincial judges.

In a brief opening statement, I summarized the anticipated testimony of the 34 witnesses to be called—13 police officers and 21 civilians.

Judge Conner, with the utmost cordiality, thanked counsel for charting the course of the Crown's case.

Civility—another good sign.

Conner's pen flew across the pages of his trial book as he recorded the words and noted the nuances of each witness.

Industry—yet another good omen; a clear acknowledgement that the judge would not deny justice through delay. The preliminary inquiry was off to a splendid start.

Recesses were brief, interruptions were infrequent and court always started on time. Conner ruled with maximum efficiency, so much so that the Crown's case was concluded at 3:20 p.m., Thursday, March 6.

The defence elected to call no evidence and court was adjourned until the following Monday.

The pressure was now on the judge. He had to make up his mind whether he would admit as evidence, or reject, John James's oral comments and the written statement he had given to Preisentanz and Gove.

Monday, March 10

Conner was at the appointed place and on time as usual.

Without preamble, he began to review the circumstances by which James had come to be interviewed by officers investigating the Adriaenssens murder. The judge observed that at all relevant times up to and after James's written statement had been obtained:

"[T]he accused was not under arrest, was not charged and cautioned, and was not advised of his rights as set forth in the Young Offenders Act and in the Canadian Charter of Rights and Freedoms. As well, the accused was not told he did not have to accompany the peace officers to the Public Safety Building, that he was free to leave the Public Safety Building, that he was not required to answer questions put to him, or why the peace officers were interviewing him.

"The peace officers testified they were interviewing the accused as a witness and that they did not suspect the accused until 10:23 p.m., after the written statement had been completed and they had left the interview room and obtained further information. Finally, the peace officers testified that the accused was free not to answer the questions put to him, was free not to make the written statement, and was free to leave the Public Safety Building at any time prior to 10:23 p.m."

Citing a decision of the highest court in the land to support his position, the judge said:

"It is clear that the Crown must prove the voluntariness of the oral and written statements of the accused before they may be admitted into evidence, whether the statements were made by the accused as a witness, suspect, or charged person and whether or not the statements were made during the early investigation of the offence."

Conner cited more judicial authorities to support his thesis and then, scarcely drawing a breath, he delivered his next sentence which occupied 19 lines of transcript:

"Notwithstanding the facts that the accused was not cautioned that he did not have to attend at the Public Safety Building and once there that he was free to leave at any time, that he did not have to answer any questions or make any statements and that if he made any comments or statements they might be used in evidence in subsequent court proceedings, that he was not advised of his right to retain and instruct counsel, that his parents or other suitable relative or adult or guardian was not asked to accompany the accused to the Public Safety Building and was not present when the accused was interviewed, and I particularly note that an adult relative was present at 89 Lorne Avenue when the peace officers asked the accused to accompany them to the Public Safety Building, and notwithstanding the nature of the interview, and the fact that the accused was at times cross-examined by the peace officers, I find the oral comments and the written statement to have been freely and voluntarily made by the operating mind of the accused."

Conner paused to catch his breath, then added: "However, the issue of the admissibility has not yet been determined."

It would be a great disservice to the learned judge to fail to state that his decision was peppered with passages from the judgments of superior courts. The relevant sections of the Young Offenders Act were scrupulously analyzed and the police officers' alleged failure to comply with them underlined again and again.

The prosecutors could hardly quarrel with Conner's synopsis of their argument.

"Crown counsel submitted that peace officers do not have

to go around advising every young person of their rights under the Young Offenders Act before speaking to them. They argue that peace officers have a right to interview people to investigate suspected offences. In support of its position that peace officers are not required to caution every person they speak with or to advise every person of their rights, Crown counsel quoted from a judgment of Mr. Justice Huband who said, in an earlier case:

"'It should be made clear that not all confessions by minors will be rendered inadmissible if a guardian has not previously been given the opportunity to retain and instruct counsel. Early in the investigation of this crime, for example, investigating officers spoke to many persons, some of them underage, in an attempt to piece together the circumstances of the crime. The accused was interviewed on two occasions, not as a suspect, but simply as a person who might know something of what had taken place when the crime was committed. Had he blurted out a confession when first spoken to, there is little doubt that it would be admissible.'"

Conner then referred to another judgment upon which the Crown relied and incorporated a passage from the polished prose of a most distinguished jurist, Mr. Justice Arthur Martin, who wrote:

"'A police officer, when he is endeavouring to discover whether or by whom an offence has been committed, is entitled to question any person, whether suspected or not, from whom he thinks that useful information can be obtained. Although a police officer is entitled to question any person in order to obtain information with respect to a suspected offence, he, as a general rule, has no power to compel the person questioned to answer. Moreover, he has no power to detain a person for questioning, and if the person questioned declines to answer, the police officer must allow him to proceed upon his way unless he arrests him on reasonable and probable grounds.'"

Again, Conner summarized the essence of the Crown's argument by saying:

"It is the position of the Crown that the accused, at the time he was being questioned by Constable Gove and Sergeant Preisentanz, was not under arrest, was not under detention, was not a suspect, and was being questioned early in the investigation of this crime in an attempt to piece together the circumstances of the crime. The peace officers were endeavouring to discover whether or by whom an offence had been committed; to obtain information with respect to a suspected offence."

In the 31 minutes that Conner spoke, he carefully expanded upon the reasons for his decision. He had found the oral comments and written statement to have been freely and voluntarily made by the operating mind of the accused. He found, however, that the investigating officers fell far short of the mark in their attempted compliance with the provisions of the Young Offenders Act.

And so, at 10:31 a.m., on a bitterly cold Monday, March 10, he dropped the first bombshell.

The statements of the accused, both oral and written, were inadmissible!

Conner had stated earlier that it was not his practice to hear the contents of written statements until he had ruled that they were voluntary.

While he had conceded that James's written statement met the test of voluntariness, the failure of the officers to comply with the spirit and the letter of the Young Offenders Act precluded its admission as evidence. Because of his ruling, the judge was unaware of what James had said in the statement.

At that point, the Crown's case hung by a tenuous thread. The outcome would depend on the judge's evaluation of the circumstantial evidence.

For the balance of the morning, Crown counsel argued for committal, the defence for discharge. Court then adjourned until 2 p.m., at which time the judge would give his decision.

Kee, the younger prosecutor, was a man of many robust appetites ordinarily, but this noonday he could only mount a half-hearted assault on an eight-ounce glass of V-8 juice.

"We're in big trouble," he moaned incessantly.

Conner resumed court at 2:10 p.m.

"He's late," muttered Kee. "A bad omen."

Again, without preamble, the judge read from his written text.

"The issue for my determination is whether there is any evidence adduced at this preliminary inquiry upon which a reasonable jury, properly instructed, could return a verdict of guilty. I am required to commit the accused for trial if there is admissible evidence which could, if it were believed, result in conviction. The evidence discloses that the accused may have had opportunity to commit the offence, he having left the Maryland Hotel shortly before or around the time the deceased left her grandmother's suite to return to her own suite. The accused returned to the deceased's apartment building which is situated 1 1/2 to two blocks from the Maryland Hotel."

Conner proceeded to summarize the evidence presented by James Cadieux, the R.C.M.P.'s hair and fibre analyst.

That testimony revealed that scalp hair consistent with Ruby's had been found on James's T-shirt and socks. As well, one scalp hair consistent with James's had been detected on each of the cinder block and the brown bag and white shroud used to cover Ruby's body. Another three scalp hairs consistent with his had been recovered from the garage floor, as had one pubic hair. Fibres consistent with those from his cap, T-shirt, sweatpants and jacket cuffs were retrieved from Ruby's body and/or her panties, overalls or T-shirt.

Conner noted that:

"Mr. Cadieux testified that the polyester fibres found on the accused's black T-shirt, the accused's black trackpants, and the accused's black leather jacket were different types of polyester fibres, each different from the other.

"He also testified that the comparison of hair and fibre samples is unlike the comparison of fingerprints in that the comparison of hair and fibre samples does not provide one hundred per cent identification and does not eliminate the possibility that the hairs came from another person. However, Mr. Cadieux stated that coincidental hair matches are very rare.

"Finally, Mr. Cadieux testified that the fibres which were compared were not rare, and that he could not exclude the possibility of the recovered fibres coming from other sources. However, he said that the combination of this finding makes the finding of consistency more probable."

The judge then offered his assessment:

"It is my conclusion from the evidence of Mr. Cadieux that a reasonable jury, properly instructed, could conclude his findings establish a high degree of probability, in fact beyond a reasonable doubt, that the accused and deceased came into contact with one another. However, the evidence does not establish when the contact took place. There is evidence that the accused was in the Gouvreau suite in the apartment building where the deceased lived, prior to going to the Maryland Hotel on the evening of September 13th, 1985. There is also evidence that the accused knew the Gouvreaus who occupied the third-floor suite at 628 1/2 Notre Dame."

Conner paused momentarily before adding quietly:

"One can hypothesize when and where and how the accused and deceased came into contact with one another, but that is not proper."

Kee leaned over.

"What the hell is that supposed to mean?" he muttered to me.

The judge was, at long last, about to share the result of his deliberations with counsel and the many others who were anxiously awaiting his decision. Most judges who have toiled in the courtroom before their elevation to the bench announce their decisions right off the bat. They remember well the anxiety and trauma they suffered with the long, slow judicial wind-up.

Conner chose to recount another self-evident truth.

"The onus is on the Crown," he declared, "to satisfy the court that there is sufficient evidence to commit the accused to stand trial. Suffice it to say that a reasonable jury, properly instructed, could not..."

"I'm going to be sick," Kee said audibly.

"...conclude beyond a reasonable doubt on the evidence

adduced before me that the accused murdered Ruby Adriaenssens..."

Then the bombshell burst.

"...and I therefore discharge him."

CHAPTER 7

"Hatred comes from the heart; contempt from the head; and neither feeling is quite within our control."
—Arthur Schopenhauer (1788–1860)

Reactions

In a flash, John James and Brenda Keyser were locked in an embrace.

Dumbfounded, Kee and I stared at the killer and his lawyer entwined in each other's arms.

"Well, gentlemen, I can tell you this," her words rebounded back. "If it had been my kid, there wouldn't even be a trial."

James later told reporters, "All I heard was 'discharged.'"

He was enjoying his newly acquired celebrity status.

"It was a complete surprise to me. I looked up at my lawyer. She said, 'Yes.' I hugged my lawyer. I wanted to scream, but the judge was there."

There is disagreement among those who witnessed the performance as to who hugged whom first, the lawyer or the client.

I turned away in disgust, overcome by gut-wrenching nausea. I walked over to a window and stood, looking out, seeing nothing.

And then the faces of old colleagues began to peer through the fog of forgotten yesterdays—Jack Powell, Maurice Arpin,

Earl Solomon, Roy Gallagher—not a saintly man among them.

There were others too with whom I had wrestled in earlier years at the bar—tough contenders who fought so hard in the old arenas of the criminal law, where the judicial referees understood the rules and enforced them, and where the penalties were so much stiffer.

The contenders played the game much differently then, with an innate sense of how it should be played.

They understood the part they had to play and had to be seen to be playing in the courts of criminal justice.

They played to win, but they took their wins and losses in stride. Even in the euphoria of victory, even at gunpoint, they couldn't embrace a killer.

As I stared glumly at the snow-laden branches of the trees on the boulevard below, my mind switched back to something Conner had said.

"One can hypothesize when and where and how the accused and deceased came into contact with one another, but that is not proper."

I thought about the circumstantial evidence—the child's scalp hairs on James's T-shirt and white socks, the clump of her head hair and a strand of his scalp hair stuck to the rough-cast cinder block, all grim reminders of the evidence that never lies.

Jurors are never instructed to hypothesize or speculate. They are told that it is open to them to draw logical inferences from proven facts. It certainly would have been open to them to have concluded that the murder took place in the garage—unless, I thought with unbridled cynicism, there had been evidence that James was in the habit of walking around town with a 50-pound building block tucked underneath his arm.

The discharge had unbolted the prison door. James was free to walk out.

"A burst of outrage from the gathered spectators" is how one reporter described reaction to the decision.[1]

James, smiling broadly, made his way past the angry people and through the courtroom door to short-lived freedom.

Several sullen-faced citizens remained behind. A well-groomed, sombre man addressed them.

"If the courts aren't going to take care of it, maybe the public should," he said as those around nodded in agreement.

Beside him was an attractive, blonde-haired, blazing-eyed young lady.

"I just wanted to start hitting him," she said, her anger scarcely under control. "I just wanted to beat him."

A third person, a sallow-faced, frail young woman in blue jeans, noted with bitterness that Ruby was only three years old.

Standing on the fringe of the crowd, the grizzly sheriff's officer repeated his prophecy to anyone who cared to listen.

"This kinda' thing keeps up and you'll see them vigilantes out. I don't want to see it, but the way things keep gettin' outta hand, it's bound to happen, sure as hell."

And what of the officer's prediction? His prophecy will be fulfilled in our time unless the crumbling structure of criminal justice is soon revamped. Until then, for so many of the people who finance the system, justice will be nothing more than a hollow word.

Years ago, a formidable Supreme Court jurist, Mr. Justice Rand, outlined the purpose of a criminal trial in one of his judgments. He stated in clear simple words what was expected of Crown counsel during the conduct of a trial. Parenthetically, perhaps, he had prepared a job description for law officers of the Crown.[2]

"It cannot be over-emphasized," Rand wrote, "that the purpose of a criminal trial is not to obtain a conviction; it is to lay before a jury what the Crown considers to be credible evidence relevant to what is alleged to be a crime. Counsel have a duty to see that all available legal proof of the facts is presented; it should be done firmly and pressed to its legitimate strength, but it must also be done fairly. The role of prosecutor excludes any notion of winning or losing; his function is a matter of public duty in which, in civil life, there can be none charged with greater personal responsibility. It is to be efficiently performed with an ingrained sense of the dignity, the seriousness and the justness of these proceedings."

This statement had become my creed. So often, down through the years, I had said to jurors at the opening of a proceeding:

"I think it is well for Crown counsel, during a trial such as this, to remind himself of the wise counsel of a former judge of the Supreme Court of Canada, Mr. Justice Rand, who said..."

Then I would share with them the coveted articles laid down by the redoubtable jurist.

But for one brief hour, I had lost faith in the administration of criminal justice. I hated the miserable creatures who had defiled it. To hell with the creed. It was a sham and it always had been.

I could pinpoint to the minute when the rupture had occurred—at precisely 2:16 p.m., Monday, March 10, 1986. It had burst when I heard the invidious words, "I therefore discharge him."

Where had my noble sense of public duty gone? Right out the door of the courtroom along with the killer.

Prosecutors, although they may be charged with greater personal responsibility, are just ordinary human beings. We love and we hate. We too shed tears for a murdered child.

And so it was, in the wake of the discharge and in despondency, I gladly would have traded my barrister's robe for a thick rope and a ride with the vigilantes.

Les Kee's face was sullen. Angrily, he crammed his notes and law reports into an oversized black briefcase.

The clerk of the court reappeared from a doorway leading to the judge's entrance.

"Judge Conner wants to see Crown counsel in his chambers," she announced.

"Well, this is one Crown counsel who doesn't want to see Judge Conner," Kee snapped.

The judge was standing behind his desk when we were ushered in.

"What was in the written statement?" he asked brusquely.

The colour drained from his face as Kee told him. Then, as suddenly as an unexpected squall, Conner lashed out at the police, pounding away at their ineptitude in interrogating the accused. The outburst had generated heat. His face resumed its normal colour, but it darkened as he angrily announced he would make it abundantly clear to the chief of police that he was not at all happy with this phase of the investigation.

Kee, an ex-cop and a friend of Anderson, Osborne, Preisentanz and Gove, listened to the tirade and bristled. So did I, having known the dedicated officers since they were police cadets.

The criticism, even from a judge, was totally unwarranted and unfair. In some quarters, however, cop-bashing has become a popular sport. Judge-bashing is a punishable offence.

The camaraderie of bench and bar enhances the joy of the practice of law.

This time there was none.

As we left the chambers, Kee put his arm around my shoulders.

"We'll get James. We'll get the bastard," he said quietly. "He's still going to face a judge and jury. Now let's move our asses over to your office and bang out a direct indictment."

I grinned as we started for the street.

"Do you figure he might be back in the bucket by midnight?"

The Direct Indictment

The Criminal Code of Canada provides that, where an accused has been discharged at the preliminary inquiry stage, an indictment may be signed by an attorney general or his deputy.

Court had adjourned at 2:16 p.m. In little over an hour, Deputy Attorney General Tanner Elton had signed his name to the new indictment.

The document effectively nullified the Conner discharge.

Soon, 12 men and women would collectively decide when and where and how the accused and deceased came into contact with one another. They wouldn't hypothesize. They would make their decision according to the evidence.

Attorney General Roland Penner returned to his office from the campaign trail around 4 p.m. His deputy minister briefed him on the details of the James discharge and the new indictment. Penner then spoke to journalists who hovered outside his office, telling them his department felt there was enough evidence against James to justify a trial.

"Even though he has been discharged at a preliminary hearing, we think there is evidence that a jury ought to consider and therefore he should go to trial. We think it's inappropriate in this case to have someone accused of a crime of this nature to be walking the streets without the larger question of his guilt or innocence decided."[3]

Penner added that his decision shouldn't be viewed as a political one during an election campaign.

"I acted on the basis of my attorneys' advice. It's not a political decision. I personally believe the case warrants a jury trial."[4]

Nobody had suggested that the preferring of the direct indictment might be perceived as having been politically motivated—nobody except the attorney general himself.

A man of tremendous accomplishment, Penner was an outstanding counsel and an effective attorney general. But, above all, he was the consummate politician.

Reporters trailed James to his sister's house during his few hours of freedom. Like a magpie, he couldn't stop chattering. He told them that he was bar-hopping the day of Ruby's murder and didn't know what the cops were talking about when they arrested him the next day.

"I hope they catch the guy that did it. Naturally everybody feels sorry for the death of a three-year-old girl."[5]

He had, he said, gone to school with Ruby's Uncle Shane.

James, who quit school in Grade 10, said he would like to

finish his education and help juveniles who are in trouble with the law.

While he jabbered, the reporters scribbled. One, striving to capture the mood of the interview, drivelled that "The slender youth, puffing on a cigarette, relaxed in a chair and quenched a long-sought craving for a bottle of Coca-Cola." (And, in order to ensure that the readers would be fully informed, it was reported that Cecil, the younger brother, had raced out to make the purchase, a two-litre bottle.)[6]

"That was good," John James said. "I missed Big Macs and pizza."

He spoke of his six months in custody.

"It was hard. Several times I thought of committing suicide. But I thought twice. God put me on earth for a purpose. My belief in God kept me going."[7]

God had put Ruby Adriaenssens on earth for a purpose too.

The wheels of justice can move, at times, with surprising swiftness. The direct indictment had been signed, an arrest warrant issued, and the killer rearrested by 8 p.m. John Thomas James Jr. was back in custody a scant six hours after Conner had released him.

CHAPTER 8

"Blessed is the man who having nothing to say, abstains from giving us wordy evidence of the fact."
—George Eliot (1819-1880)

The Quest for Loopholes

"Obviously he is really disappointed about the speed with which he was picked up," Brenda Keyser told reporters after her client's arraignment before Mr. Justice Daniel Kennedy in the Court of Queen's Bench the following morning.[1]

She expressed surprise at the speed with which the direct indictment was drawn up.

"You wonder how much reflection went into the decision when the indictment comes out that quickly. They didn't let moss grow on the (Conner) judgment."

Kennedy fixed the date for James's début before judge and jury: Monday, April 21. The trial would get under way within 41 days—unless a legal loophole could be found.

Ferret-like lawyers have always searched and combed the tangled underbrush of the criminal law, seeking for their clients a lawful escape route from criminal responsibility. The hunt, in this case, had only just begun.

Keyser could never contain her irresistible impulse to keep the media informed of her every move in the course of her client's defence. She announced that she would be applying for bail for James, noting that the Conner decision would give weight to her request.

But on Friday, March 14, bail was denied.

Following that unsuccessful application, Keyser informed reporters that she intended to challenge the direct indictment on jurisdictional grounds.

Wednesday, April 2, 1986

Keyser appeared before Madam Justice Ruth Krindle of the Court of Queen's Bench seeking a writ of *certiorari*.

Lawyers have been begging for indulgences from courts via this prescriptive device since the sixteenth century. Such a writ may issue from a superior court upon the complaint of a party that he has not received justice in an inferior court.

John James would get no such indulgence from Krindle, whose short, incisive judgment so declared.

After recounting the legal steps that had led to James's transfer to adult court, his discharge after a preliminary hearing and his rearrest, Krindle wrote:

"Counsel argues that the effect of the discharge was to end the transfer order and the jurisdiction of the adult court over the accused with respect to the offence. I do not agree. The limitations placed on the jurisdiction conferred by the transfer order are set out in the Young Offenders Act:

"(a) the accused can only be proceeded against in adult court in accordance with the law ordinarily applicable to an adult charged with that offence; and

"(b) the jurisdiction conferred on the adult court lies in respect only of the offence referred to in the transfer order or an included offence.

"Those are the only limitations on the jurisdiction of the adult court once the youth has been validly transferred.

"An adult charged with the offence of murder, in accordance with the law ordinarily applicable, may be subject to an indictment for that offence preferred with the consent of the attorney general, notwithstanding that a provincial judge may have found there to be insufficient evidence on that charge to bind the adult over for trial.

"The procedure which was followed in the present case is in accordance with the law ordinarily applicable to an adult charged with an indictable offence. The direct indictment does not therefore exceed the jurisdictional limitation on the adult court, which limitation is implicit in the act. As well, because the offence charged in the direct indictment is the same offence as that referred to in the transfer order, there can be no suggestion that the limitations in the act have been exceeded.

"I find that the court has jurisdiction to proceed on the direct indictment and that the transfer order confers that jurisdiction.

"The application for *certiorari* is accordingly dismissed."

Monday, April 14

Defence counsel's search for a hole through which the killer could crawl his way to freedom was relentless. For the second time in as many weeks Keyser stood before Krindle asking that the murder charge be thrown out.

During this attempt, counsel contended that, contrary to the provisions of the Young Offenders Act, Youth Court Judge Larry Ring had failed to read the charge to the accused when he first appeared before the court on September 16, 1985. As a result of the judge's failure, she argued, all subsequent proceedings were null and void.

"What is the Crown's position?" Krindle asked.

The reply was succinct:

"The motion is without merit and should be denied, my lady. The section of the act upon which my learned friend relies was designed to protect unrepresented youth, not those who have defence lawyers present and who are fully informed. It is most inappropriate for Ms. Keyser to now ask that proceedings against her client be declared a nullity when she, herself, had been in court with John James and had failed to request that the charge be read to her client in the first place."

If it can be said that certain judges acquire their own trademark, then Krindle's was unique. Hers was a warm and lovely smile. As always, she smiled at counsel as she thanked them for their submissions. She then reserved judgment on the defence motion.

This time, Keyser had tried to find an escape hatch for her client through a well-constructed section of the Young Offenders Act, Section 12. It provides, simply, that:

"12(1) Where a young person against whom an information is laid first appears before a youth court judge, the judge shall

(a) cause the information to be read to him; and

(b) where the young person is not represented by counsel, inform him

of his right to be so represented."

Thursday, April 17

Again, the ruling was brief and pointed.

"I am not satisfied," Krindle began, "that the directions of Section 12(1) of the Young Offenders Act go to the very jurisdiction of the court to deal with a young person in respect of an offence charged. I am therefore not satisfied that the failure by the court to comply with the directions set forth in Section 12(1), within the time constraints referred to in that section, would be such as to deprive the court of jurisdiction to deal with the charge and would thereby render all proceedings subsequent to that failure nullities. The very fact that the section itself permits counsel to waive the requirement of Section 12(1)a, in my opinion, reinforces this position.

"In any event, I am satisfied that the conduct of counsel, both on the first appearance and subsequent thereto, has amounted to a waiver within the meaning of Section 12(2) which provides that a young person may waive the requirement of the reading of the information when he or she is represented by counsel. In that regard, it is noteworthy that, on first appearance in youth court, the accused was represented by counsel, the same counsel who represents him to this day."

Krindle quoted in full the record of James's first court appearance and concluded that the transcript of the proceedings spoke for itself.

"Following that appearance," she continued, "there was a series of remands and ultimately a transfer hearing. No issue was taken in youth court at any time as to loss of jurisdiction arising from non-compliance with Section 12(1)a). A transfer order was granted and a full preliminary inquiry was held in adult court. No issue was raised at the preliminary inquiry stage as to the jurisdiction of the youth court to transfer the youth by virtue of its non-compliance with Section 12(1)a). Now, at the eleventh hour, one week before the commencement of a trial before a judge and jury on the allegation in question, a motion is brought alleging that nine months ago the youth court lost jurisdiction over this matter by failing to comply on first appearance with Section 12(1)a) and therefore all subsequent proceedings have been null and void.

"For the reasons aforesaid, I find that there was no loss of jurisdiction by the youth court following the first appearance. The transfer order cannot be attacked on that ground.

"The motion is disallowed."

The search for a fatal technical flaw had been futile. Keyser just couldn't find a loophole. The case against her client would proceed to trial on its merits.

CHAPTER 9

"Our civilization has decided, and very justly decided, that determining the guilt or innocence of men is a thing too important to be trusted to trained men. If it wishes for light upon that awful matter, it asks men who know no more law than I know, but who can feel the things that I felt in the jury box. When it wants a library catalogued, or the solar system discovered, or any trifle of that kind, it uses up its specialists. But when it wishes anything done that is really serious, it collects twelve of the ordinary men standing about. The same thing was done, if I remember right, by the founder of Christianity."
—Gilbert K. Chesterton (1874-1936)

Picking the Jury

"Juror, look at the prisoner. Prisoner, look at the juror," commands the clerk of the court.

Lawyers, most of whom wear glasses, are the major players in this hit-and-miss game of selection and rejection. They squint and stare at each candidate. Like phrenologists who theorize that the shape of the skull reveals a person's mind and character, the lawyers gape and gawk and crane their necks to scan the subject for a flaw or fatal defect, some tell-tale sign—a shifty eye or nervous tic; emaciated or overfed; much too young or far too old; unkempt or too slick by half; prissy.

Counsel are furnished with a copy of the jury list before court commences. Then, ill-equipped with such scanty, raw intelligence as the names, addresses and occupations of potential jurors, they challenge and stand aside indiscriminately, heedlessly displaying their vile prejudices (no Slavs or Asians or Blacks) and their baseless misconceptions (retired: probably senile) and effecting the inevitable, iniquitous rejection of the resident of dilapidated Magnus Avenue (more likely than not has a criminal record).

How can the basic nature of man be thus discovered on such a cursory inspection? How can this glimpse reveal some latent mental deficiency or the incapacity to keep an open mind until all of the evidence has been presented?

Rare indeed is the advocate who is content with the first 12 citizens called to sit in judgment of the prisoner in the dock.

Most, unfortunately, pick and poke like bargain-hunters at a rummage sale and reject until the entire jury panel is exhausted.

This cumbersome, tedious and frustrating mode of assembling 12 triers of the facts survives, as it has through the ages, unaltered—absurd perhaps, but as entrenched in the fabric of trial by jury as the presumption of innocence itself. It is, for some lawyers, one of the very cornerstones of democracy; for others, it's a real pain in the ass.

The Trial: Monday, April 21, 1986

As each juror "came to the book" to be sworn, the clerk of the court recited in a dreadful monotone the archaic words of the juror's oath:

"You shall well and truly try and true deliverance make between our Sovereign Lady the Queen and the prisoner at the bar, whom you shall have in charge, and a true verdict give...," she chanted sombrely, and then, with an unexpected and elaborate flourish, she sang out the balance: "...according to the evidence."

Her strident cadenza lent, she no doubt reckoned, to the awesomeness of a high court criminal trial.

"I will," each bemused juror promised tentatively.

Counsel had speculated that it would take at least two days to empanel a jury. To their surprise, the twelfth juror was sworn at 11:12 a.m., just 72 minutes after the opening of the spring assize.

The solemn ritual of trial by judge and jury was about to begin.

"Prisoner," cried the clerk, "please stand up.

"You stand charged by the name of John Thomas James, Jr."

The clerk then read from the indictment:

"John Thomas James Jr. stands charged that he, the said John Thomas James Jr. on or about the thirteenth day of September, in the year of our Lord, one thousand nine hundred and eighty-five, at or near the City of Winnipeg, in the Province of Manitoba, did unlawfully commit first degree murder on the person of Ruby Adriaenssens.

"How say you, guilty or not guilty?"

"Not guilty," James snapped.

"Hearken to your plea as the court records it. You say you are not guilty?"

"Yes, I do," the prisoner spat defiantly.

The jurors sat stiffly, waiting tensely for what they knew not, in an unfamiliar place, where the language was so strange: "Hearken to your plea...true deliverance make...whom you shall have in charge...a true verdict give."

Madam Justice Krindle, perched above them on the dais to their left, seemed so tiny and so young to be a judge.

She leaned forward, her arms extended and fingers entwined. Turning slightly to her right, she looked into the 12 grim faces before her. And then she smiled at them with her magical smile.

Some judges read their opening remarks from a prepared text, often evincing their uncertainties with an irritating, raspy clearing of the throat. Awkward attempts to direct jurors on the parts they must play when the curtain goes up frequently flop miserably.

Ruth Krindle is one of those uncommon jurists who speak easily to the chicken farmer and to the telephone operator and to the man who moves the heavy equipment. Her eyes never stray from the faces of the jurors as she addresses them. They listen to her and they understand what she is saying. They like her. She quickly gains their respect. Before the end of a trial, she has shared a lot of herself with them—her knowledge, her wisdom and her good humour—and they, with her, their admiration and, sometimes, as in the case of Her Majesty the Queen versus John Thomas James Jr., their affection as well.

"Members of the jury," Krindle began as she leaned back, comfortably dwarfed in her high-backed chair, "now that you have been sworn, you 12 jurors, together with myself, constitute the court that will try this case. To that extent, you become, along with me, judges of the Court of Queen's Bench for the duration of this trial. You are solely responsible for the determination of the facts. I am responsible for directing you and counsel as to the law, and, in that respect, what I say as to the law is binding on you and counsel.

"Within our field of responsibility, you the jury and I as presiding judge have exclusive jurisdiction. As to your responsibility, you are to understand that nothing becomes a fact until you find it to be so. It is therefore of the utmost importance that you follow the evidence carefully, and, in so doing, form your impression of the witnesses. Some witnesses will impress you as being impartial, fair, credible; others may have a vested interest of some sort in the outcome of the case. That's a factor to be borne in mind when assessing whether you can believe all, or part, or none of what a particular witness testifies to. There may be discrepancies in a witness's testimony. If there are, and it happens frequently, you will have to determine whether what you have heard is as a result of a witness relying on memory and making an honest mistake, which can easily occur, or whether it was a deliberate falsehood. Listen carefully and observe the demeanour of each witness as he or she is giving testimony.

"In addition to the oral evidence, there may be documents, photographs or other tangible things introduced as exhibits in the trial. You will have an opportunity to consider these as they are brought forward, and they will ultimately go with you into the jury room when you retire to consider your verdict.

"You are to take nothing into consideration that is not presented to you as evidence in this trial. If you have read or heard anything about this case before coming to court, and I expect you have, then you are to banish it from your minds. If anyone other than a fellow juror should try to speak to you about this case during the trial, report the occurrence to the sheriff at once and we will deal with it. It is extremely important that you banish from your mind any preconceptions which you may have had about this case before the trial started. It is necessary that the accused be tried on the evidence that you will hear in this courtroom and on nothing else.

"People may approach you out of the courtroom and try to discuss the case with you. I advise you not to discuss it, not even with your family and your friends. Comments could be made by people that might affect your independent judgment. If the subject is raised—and I have no doubt that it will be, your family is going to want to know what you were doing all day— simply tell them that you cannot discuss the case; the judge has instructed you not to discuss it. Blame it on me, okay?"

Twelve grins, 12 affirmative nods, but not one among them was ever going to blame this, or anything else, on the tiny, friendly judge.

She had some advice for them with regard to newspaper and television reports.

"Please try not to read or listen to those stories," she asked. "The reporters are in and out of this courtroom during the course of the trial. They cover not just what is going on in this courtroom, but what is going on in other courtrooms as well. The editors, who decide what to print and how to print it and what headlines to run, are not in this courtroom during the course of the trial. Your collective recollection and your collective response to the evidence is likely to be far more accurate and balanced than anything you may read, see or hear in the media. In order to be not influenced by it, may I suggest you simply avoid, to the extent that you possibly can, reading or listening to the media reports.

"It is important that you keep an open mind about this case until the last word has been said. The evidence will be laid before us, bit by bit, rather like constructing a building; and it isn't until all of the pieces have been put before us that you will be able to judge what sort of structure has been created."

The 12 new acolytes were motionless and wide-eyed, engrossed in the young judge's instructional discourse. She had cast a spell over them, I mused.

"Now, as to the procedure that is followed in a criminal trial. When I have concluded these opening instructions, I will invite counsel for the Crown," Krindle said as she motioned to me, "to introduce the case to you. He is assisted by Mr. Les Kee. In so doing, he will state what he expects the evidence for the Crown will be. You must always bear in mind that his address is not evidence; it is only given to assist you in following the evidence which will be given from the witness box.

"When Crown counsel has finished his opening address, he will proceed to call witnesses and question them. When he has finished his questioning of a witness, Ms. Keyser, assisted by Mr. Baragar, who are seated at counsel table closest to you, will have the opportunity of cross-examining the Crown witnesses. The purpose of cross-examination is to test the evidence given by the witness in chief, and sometimes to bring out new facts.

"When counsel for the Crown has called all the witnesses he intends to call in support of the Crown's case, counsel for the accused will have the right to make an opening statement to you if she so desires, and to call such witnesses as she may think proper. Any witness that counsel for the accused calls is, of course, subject to cross-examination by counsel for the Crown."

Jurors are often confused by judges who try to explain their necessary exclusion from the courtroom during legal argument. Krindle made it sound so logical.

"From time to time," she told them, "a question will arise as to whether certain matters are admissible as evidence in this case. When counsel get to a point in the case where such matters are about to arise, they will indicate to me that they will need a legal ruling as to the admissibility of evidence. Such a situation is handled in this way. I will ask you to retire to your jury room while I listen, in your absence, to what is proposed to be put before the court as evidence. If I come to the conclusion that it offends the law of admissibility, you will not hear it and it will not form any part of what you have to consider. On the other hand, if I decide, as a matter of law, that evidence is properly admissible, when you are recalled from your jury room it will be given in evidence before you and form part of the evidence in this case. I am advised by counsel that, at least on one occasion, there is going to be such a request that you leave the courtroom, and that occasion will take about two or three days. What will happen in that particular instance is that counsel will give their best estimate and we will just excuse you for those two or three days. You certainly are not going to have to spend two or three days sitting in the jury room. I do not know when we will hit the point of breaking for that particular trial within a trial. You can be sure that you will hear all of the evidence that I rule to be legally admissible. You will not be troubled with the evidence that I rule to be legally inadmissible."

I had always been astounded by the amount of water that some judges, particularly the less confident ones, drank while addressing a jury. Krindle had progressed this far in her remarks having taken just one dainty sip.

Almost as an afterthought, she asked the jurors not to go to the scene of the crime.

"Do not try to gather your own evidence in any way," she cautioned. "Please do not make your own out-of-court inquiries. Insofar as the scene of the crime is concerned, among other things, it has changed somewhat since the time of the crime. But, in any event, don't make out-of-court inquiries; your verdict has got to be based on what you hear in this courtroom and nothing else."

She told them that there were just a few more things that she must mention.

"When all of the evidence has been heard, then counsel for the Crown and counsel for the accused will present their arguments to you," she said. "Again, as in the opening statement that Crown counsel is about to give you, those addresses or arguments are not evidence. They are arguments based on evidence; they are intended to assist you in applying the evidence to the issues in this case.

"When counsel have addressed you, then I must deliver my charge to you as to the law. In doing so, I will comment on the evidence that impresses me as being important. What I may say as to the evidence is not binding on you any more than what counsel may say as to evidence. It is only the expression of one or more points of view. When I finish my charge, it will then be time for you to retire and consider your verdict."

The judge may have made notes in preparation for her remarks. If so, she did not refer to them. Her delivery was free and easy and almost as informal as a fireside chat. Skilfully, she was conditioning the jurors for the formidable task upon which they were about to embark, one of the toughest jobs a democratic society imposes upon its members—to sit in judgment of a fellow citizen charged with murder.

During the selection process, Krindle had asked each prospective juror if, given the emotion and media attention involved in the case, he or she could put aside preconceived ideas and deliver a verdict based on the evidence in court. More than a dozen had acknowledged their inability to give John James a fair hearing. She had excused them. Another 15 had been rejected by counsel for both the Crown and defence.

The 12 who had been chosen were now ready to assume, together with the young and tiny jurist, their roles as judges of the Court of Queen's Bench for the duration of the trial.

Another smile, a word or two about the hours that the court would sit each day, Krindle's educated guess as to the length of the trial, and, finally, the invitation to Crown counsel to make his opening statement.

It was only then, I noticed out of the corner of my eye as I walked toward the jury box, that the judge took her second sip of water.

Even though James had confessed to sexually violating and murdering the child, no reference could be made in the opening statement to any admission of guilt. Conceivably, his confession could be ruled inadmissible. For that reason, I felt rather emasculated as I droned on for 35 dreary minutes that morning.

I subjected the jurors to back-to-back, nutshell accounts of the anticipated testimony of 32 prosecution witnesses—a blunder, I realized in retrospect. I was grateful that no one had squirmed or fidgeted or yawned while I spoke.

Dejectedly, I left the courtroom, reproaching myself for not having simply said, as I had initially intended:

"John Thomas James Jr. plucked a tiny bud from its tender vine. The evidence will reveal that he crushed it and discarded it. It would never blossom forth as a lovely rose. He destroyed something of inestimable and indescribable beauty.

"For this, he must be locked in darkness for the rest of his days."

They stream into the courtroom where the prisoner is about to be tried for murder. Some foredoom his fate. Some look sullen, even hostile.

The ambient air is tension-laden.

The lawyers' faces are taut; those of the spectators reflect a mosaic of many moods—fear, hatred, anger, sorrow.

Security is tight.

The first witness for the prosecution, the affable giant Craig Boan, eclipsed the clerk of the court as she ushered him into the witness box shortly after the session resumed at 2 p.m.

Boan quickly assumed the shape of a large walking cane by dropping his head and shoulders forward and downward. The clerk extended herself on tiptoe and thrust the Bible into his right hand so that he might be sworn.

The story of a beautiful little girl, slain more than seven months before, was at last about to be heard by a jury.

When a relative or friend of the accused is subpoenaed to give evidence on behalf of the prosecution in a murder trial, Crown counsel may have to contend with a hostile witness.

Frequently, friends of the deceased and family members respond to defence counsel's questions on cross-examination with contempt, even venomously.

This trial, in some respects, was unique.

The Crown did call relatives and friends of the prisoner—Harry James, Sharon Louise James, Ferlon Goosehead and Corrine Demas. None could have been more forthright and candid. There wasn't a trace of animosity. They all showed uncommon courtesy.

Four members of the Adriaenssens family testified on behalf of the prosecution—the murdered child's mother Kim, her grandmother Shirley, her Aunt Tania and Uncle Shane. They spoke in anguish, but without bitterness. Defence counsel saw fit to ask nothing of the bereaved. Had she put questions to those gentle and wounded people, they would have responded with dignity and deference.

This case, unlike most murder trials, was devoid of moments of high drama. There was an ever-present solemnity during the proceedings. The little girl's presence permeated the courtroom and dominated throughout the entire trial.

The jurors saw the living, laughing, lively child. They shuddered as Dr. Peter Markesteyn portrayed her gruesome death.

In 1976, the Law Reform Commission of Canada described the criminal trial as "a sort of morality play for all of us; a kind of public theatre in the round."

No rogues appeared before Krindle, just 32 ordinary, decent people united by a common bond—a mutual revulsion for the crime, and hearts that ached for Ruby's family.

And so it was that 32 good people testified without rancour. None attempted to shade or distort the evidence. There were no acrimonious exchanges among counsel and the witnesses.

The Ruling on Admissibility of the Accused's Statements

The judge had to decide just how much of what James told police officers was legally admissible and could be recounted to the jurors.

On April 24 and 25, the fourth and fifth days of the trial, Krindle heard in the jury's absence the testimony of Sergeants Preisentanz and Anderson, Constable Osborne, former constable Gove and Harry James. Then, she listened patiently to the submissions of three loquacious lawyers, each of whom had his or her own interpretation of parts of Section 56 of the Young Offenders Act.

After having advanced one of those legal arguments myself, I recalled an observation of that most excellent and erudite jurist, the Honourable Mr. Justice John Ambrose Scollin, who declared that "Lawyers have danced too long at the nit-pickers' ball."

The *voir dire*, the "trial within a trial" to determine the admissibility of the impugned statements, mercifully ran its course and Krindle promised to present her ruling first thing Monday morning, April 28.

The judge had been a Crown attorney. She had experienced the frustrations of sitting through interminable judicial preambles before the decision was announced. She preferred that counsel not suffer needlessly.

"Dealing with the matters raised in the *voir dire*," Krindle began, "there is nothing in the manner or the timing of the seizure of the exhibits from the person of the accused which would, in my opinion, preclude their admissibility as exhibits.

"Insofar as the comments are concerned, the comments made by the accused to the police officers up to and inclusive of the accused exercising his right to counsel, I find to be admissible.

"The comments thereafter, I rule to be inadmissible.

"A brief set of reasons for this ruling is in the process of being typed. I will be distributing it to you in court either later today or tomorrow.

"The cut-off point is the point at which, sitting in the room with Mr. James, the accused exercised his right to counsel."

It had taken two minutes. Court was adjourned at 9:32 a.m. It would reconvene at 10 o'clock.

In the circulated reasons for her ruling, Krindle wrote:

"I was favourably impressed with the demeanour of the police witnesses called on the *voir dire*.

"Ms. Keyser has attempted to make something out of the manner of questioning and to argue that the police suspected James all along. I don't accept her position. In the first place, their manner of questioning was reasonable in these circumstances."

Clearly, the judge was in the officers' corner. She possessed, unlike many of her Queen's Bench brothers and others in the courts above and below her, the capacity to understand and appreciate the police role in these and other difficult circumstances.

In her formative days in the Crown office, she had worked in the bastille-like grey building that houses police headquarters and the city's criminal courts.

Two immortal detective sergeants, the legendary Peter VanderGraaf and Jack Taylor, had assumed the dual roles of mentors and protectors to the animated youngster with the big grin who had virtually infiltrated the detective division.

She rode with them through the streets of a thousand sorrows, down alleys where human vermin squirmed, and past the "lower track" where solitary hookers hawked their wares.

From her vantage point in the rear seat of a police cruiser, she stared out at the naked city by night.

In her judgment, Krindle stated she was "satisfied beyond any reasonable doubt that all comments made by the accused to the police, both before and after the arrest of the accused, were voluntary. I am satisfied beyond any reasonable doubt that once the accused became suspected of this crime, the police complied fully with the provisions of the Charter of Rights.

"If there was a failure on the part of the police, it did not go to the issue of the charter's compliance or voluntariness. It related to the provisions of the Young Offenders Act only.

"I find that Section 56 of the act does not purport to govern the admissibility of statements made by members of the public to the police in situations where those members of the public are neither suspected nor accused of having committed a crime.

"Once the accused became a suspect, compliance with the provisions of Section 56 then, in my opinion, became mandatory, although I must confess to having some problem with the wording of certain parts of the section. Why a young person, for example, would need to be cautioned about a statement being used as evidence 'against him' when the law is clear that a statement, once admitted, is evidence both for and against an accused, is somewhat bewildering. Such a caution could perhaps mislead. I, too, confess to sharing with the police officers a degree of bewilderment about their on-going obligation to continue to acquaint the young person with his rights once he has exercised his right to counsel. I cannot accept defence counsel's suggestion that the police have an obligation to start warning youths, not only as to the potential use of their comments as evidence, but also as to the liability of a young person to be the subject of a transfer proceeding. I do not know whether the obligation of the police to acquaint young suspects with their legal rights continues after they have exercised their right to counsel and have presumably been instructed by a lawyer. I prefer to err on the side of an abundance of caution and exclude the comments made after the accused saw counsel.

"Having regard to all of the findings aforesaid, I am ruling as being admissible all comments to and inclusive of the point where the accused exercised his right to counsel. I am excluding all comments thereafter, notwithstanding that I find those comments to be voluntary and to be in compliance with the charter.

"I find as well, that while those excluded comments may not comply with the Young Offenders Act, they were taken by the police in good faith and were not the result of any deliberate disregard of the legislation by the police."

*   *   *

Leslie Hamilton Kee usually walks tall. Sometimes he struts. On that mournful April noonday, though, his butt was no more than three feet off the pavement as we headed up Kennedy Street to The Keg for lunch.

The hostess led us to a booth in a dimly lit corner of the restaurant, out of earshot of patrons who would be spared Kee's profane monologue.

He had been a cop, and a good one, for more than a dozen years. He was a strapping 16-year-old from Stonewall, Manitoba, when he was sworn in as a Winnipeg Police cadet on September 30, 1963. His arrest record as a street cop and robbery/homicide detective had satisfied him, but, as he once confided to me, "The bureaucratic bullshit was getting too heavy, so I decided to get out and go to law school."

After graduation, he was appointed Crown attorney and, in no time, was running a stable of young prosecutors in the juvenile court system, an assignment he handled innovatively for several years. During that time, he witnessed the demise of the Juvenile Delinquents Act and the creation of the Young Offenders Act.

"The old act was just fine," he said dejectedly. "All it needed was a bit of fine-tuning."

He, like many others consulted about the new legislation, had voiced concern over the consequences of the Young Offenders Act becoming law.

He slouched, his chin resting on his chest.

"I can't blame Ruth Krindle. She did the best she could with the bloody law that binds her. But don't you see what this does to our case? The jury gets to hear all about Eli Tacan, but not a goddamned word that the killer said to Angus or Cal about how he snatched the little kid off the stairs and how he used her and how he killed her.

"Christ," he exploded, "the jury won't even learn that James led Anderson and Osborne to the very spot where he killed her.

"Those assholes," he hissed as he jabbed his fork into the chef's salad and speared a lettuce leaf. "Those assholes in Ottawa. They have all the answers. Except none of them who participated in the construction of this comedy of errors they call the Young Offenders Act ever took a ride in the ass end of a police car. Worse still, none of these anaemic academics ever argued a criminal case outside a lecture hall in their lives."

"We'll get him, Les," I promised as we waited for the light at Vaughan Street.

That afternoon, Preisentanz, Gove, Anderson and Osborne shared with the jurors as much of John James's conversations and comments as the court's ruling would permit.

Then, Eli Tacan took the stand. The soft-spoken, thoughtful man quickly dispelled any notions as to his complicity in the child's murder and, in the process, exposed the accused as a blatant liar.

Tuesday, April 29

The effect of Krindle's ruling on the *voir dire* weakened the Crown's case in that damaging admissions by the accused could not be introduced as evidence. Nevertheless, I remained undaunted. The jury had yet to feel the powerful impact of the testimony of the two scientists from the crime lab, the remaining witnesses for the prosecution.

I remembered what that modern Sherlock Holmes, Herbert Leon MacDonell, had said about physical evidence:

"You can lead a jury to the truth, but you can't make them believe it. Physical evidence cannot be intimidated. It does not forget. It doesn't get excited at the moment something is happening—like people do. It sits there and waits to be detected, preserved, evaluated, and explained. This is what physical evidence is all about. In the course of a trial, defence and prosecuting attorneys may lie, witnesses may lie, the defendant certainly may lie. Even the judge may lie. Only the evidence never lies."[1]

Wayne Bellingham had detected and preserved the vital hairs and fibres that were evaluated and explained by James Cadieux.

As expected, defence counsel called no evidence on behalf of the accused. Her trial strategy had been very simple—make the Crown prove its case beyond a reasonable doubt, if it could.

When no testimony is presented on the prisoner's behalf, Crown counsel must precede counsel for the accused in final argument.

I was invited by Krindle to make my submission to the jury the next morning at 10 o'clock sharp.

I left the courtroom in a mood of subdued optimism.

John Thomas James Jr., I was satisfied, would be convicted of murder in the first degree.

The evidence never lies.

CHAPTER 10

The Prosecutor's Closing Address

I rose from the chair, bowed slightly and began softly, "May it please my lady." I addressed the 12 judges of the facts in the same quiet voice: "Ladies and gentlemen of the jury—"

I then abruptly left my lectern, moved rapidly across the floor, and stood directly behind the table that housed the exhibits. The table was no more than 10 feet from the jury and in full view.

I made no attempt to curb a welling anger. I felt flushed and taut. I saw the face of the beautiful child. My heart ached for Kim who sat alone in the back of the courtroom, frail and devastated, unable yet to accept that James alone was responsible for Ruby's death and that she, Ruby's protector, did not share blame because she had sought a few hours of personal enjoyment that fateful evening.

"The accused, John Thomas James Jr., smashed three-year-old Ruby Adriaenssens' head against this 50-pound cinder block!" I snarled as I drove my right fist against the block's jagged surface. My voice was raw.

"He fractured her skull and tore her brain and broke her neck!"

I paused; my voice softened. "And, almost instantaneously, her little heart stopped beating forever.

"The evidence in this case is overwhelmingly consistent with the guilt of the accused, and overwhelmingly inconsistent with any other rational conclusion; so much so, I say to you that, were it not my duty to advance the position of the Crown, I would go and sit down right now."

I turned away slowly and walked to the far side of the room, struggling to restrain the intensity of the anger, a hostility I had never before felt toward a prisoner in the dock. Had I gone to excess? Had I permitted personal feelings to overshadow the duty I owed the court to perform my function fairly and with an ingrained sense of the dignity and seriousness of the proceedings?

I resumed my submission in a modulated voice.

"An eminent Canadian jurist, the late Mr. Justice McInnes, said that 'there is, too often, a misconception as to the purpose of a criminal trial. It is sometimes regarded as a contest between the person making the complaint and the person accused, or between the police officer or prosecutor who is conducting the prosecution and the accused person. This is far from the truth. What we are all seeking, and what we must be seeking, is the truth of what actually occurred; and so a criminal trial is not really a contest at all. It is, more properly, a solemn inquiry, conducted under certain specific rules, whereby it is sought to ascertain the truth of what actually occurred.'

"And it is for you, the ladies and gentlemen of the jury, to ascertain the truth about what actually occurred shortly after eight o'clock on the evening of Friday, September 13th, 1985 in the garage at the rear of 695 Sherbrook Street when Ruby Adriaenssens was killed.

"Further, it is for you to ascertain the truth about what transpired subsequent to the death insofar as both the victim and the accused were concerned."

The anger had subsided, for the moment at least. Now it was as if I were chatting with friends.

"No, I didn't go to church last Sunday morning. Instead, I was sitting at home reflecting upon what I was going to say to you when I spoke to you later in the week. And I did something that I always do before I have the privilege of addressing the ladies and gentlemen of a jury. I went to a bookshelf and I took down a wonderful book that a dear old deputy attorney general gave to me when I was a young fellow starting out. It was written by a celebrated trial lawyer and one of the chapters is entitled 'The Mind of the Juror.'

"If I may, I'd like to share with you a couple of paragraphs, because, for me, they certainly sum up the juror's difficult task.

"'Jurors are expected to discover not only the errors or the perjury of witnesses, but also the errors and fallacy of the lawyers, which are even more puzzling; and it thus clearly appears that the most difficult work in the courtroom is given to the jurors. The proceedings are conducted on the assumption that the juror's knowledge, shrewdness, mental power and agility, experience in affairs, knowledge of human nature and his sense of honour will lead him to decide correctly which contestant is right and which lawyer is correct in all kinds of the most complicated controversies.

"'It is the wise juror's business to come into court and sit quietly and to say nothing, and to hear the witnesses and the arguments of the lawyers, and to decide on which side there is an abundance of proof. Notwithstanding the conflicting and the plausible but directly opposed arguments of skilful lawyers, he is expected to render a correct verdict. When the juror's task is thus described, it is plain to see that his task is far from an easy one.'

"I have watched you, ladies and gentlemen, during the course of the past few days. The close attention that you paid to the testimony of all of the witnesses is most gratifying. And I am satisfied that each and every one of you is equal to the difficult task to which you have been assigned."

I reminded the jurors that my address was not to be treated as evidence but, rather, as the Crown's interpretation of what had been revealed by witnesses during the trial.

I then turned to the substance of the case, beginning with the testimony that dealt with certain specific elements that must be proven by the Crown, namely: the victim was indeed Ruby Adriaenssens; she was an otherwise healthy child who died as a result of extensive head injuries consistent with blunt trauma;

her death occurred at almost the same time as when the force that caused the trauma was applied; and, she died on or about September 13, 1985 in the garage behind 695 Sherbrook Street in Winnipeg.

Another specific element in the charge of murder that the Crown must prove is the identity of the accused.

"In the case before you," I argued, "it seems almost ludicrous for me to touch on this aspect of proof because of the overwhelming evidence implicating John Thomas James Jr. in the violent killing of Ruby Adriaenssens.

"And who placed John Thomas James Jr. at the scene of the alleged crime? The one and only eyewitness to this unlawful killing—James himself! Yes, right out of his own mouth!

"You will well recall Sergeant Anderson's testimony:

"'Do you remember anything at all about a little girl?' he asked.

"James replied:

"'Yes, I grabbed her. I took her to a garage down the lane.'

"And in that garage," I continued, "the accused virtually left his calling cards—a hair from his head on the cinder block, hairs from his head on the garage floor—yes, even one of his pubic hairs.

"The accused not only told the police that he took the child to the garage, but he left evidence corroborating, that is, confirming, this fact."

There is a third specific ingredient to be proved in the charge of murder and that is whether the matter at hand involves an unlawful killing, a culpable or blameworthy killing.

I told the jury I did not propose to deal with this element at length "because, if ever there was a case of an unlawful killing, this is it! Obviously James did not kill the child accidentally.

"There was no provocation for this unlawful killing. James's life was not in jeopardy. He sexually attacked and brutally killed a defenceless, 25-pound, three-year-old girl.

"There is no defence.... No, this brutal killing was not accidental; nor was it prompted by provocation on the part of the deceased. The killing of the child required deliberate and intentional action on the part of the accused.

"In most cases of murder...the Crown must prove an intention to kill. However, in this case, the Crown does not have to prove that the accused formed the intent to kill Ruby Adriaenssens.

"My lady will tell you, I am certain, that murder is first degree murder in respect of a person when the death is caused by that person while committing or attempting to commit a sexual assault.

"John James killed the child while he was sexually assaulting her, ladies and gentlemen—and that constitutes first degree murder."

My knuckles were as white as the cuffs of my shirt which showed beneath the sleeves of my black barrister's vest. I again spoke in anger and with bitterness.

"Now I do not suggest for one moment that the accused took the little girl to the garage with the intention of killing her.

"No, he took her there for the sole purpose of gratifying his insidious sexual lust; the despicable gratification of his vile lust of the flesh. That was the reason he took the little girl there!

"He sexually molested her, he sexually attacked her; and during the brutal sexual assault, he killed her.... And that, I submit...is first degree murder."

I sipped a glass of ice water secreted beneath the shelf of my lectern, then trekked back in front of the jury box, seldom stopping in one place for more than a minute.

"Dr. Markesteyn told you that there were bruises around the child's rectum, peri-mortem injuries; that is, injuries that occurred around the time of death because, he observed, there was no rupture there. He stated that it was impossible to say whether the bruising occurred just before death, at death, or shortly thereafter, but certainly very shortly thereafter because, after a while, there is no more blood in the skin to cause bruising.

"Please remember that the doctor stated that the injuries were consistent with injuries which could have been caused during a sexual attack.

"And then you will recall, I know, the testimony of Dr. Kenneth McRae, the kindly specialist in the field of pediatrics and the director of the Child Protection Centre at the Children's Hospital....

"He testified...that, around the anus, extending about a two-centimetre distance, was an even area of bruising in a circumferential manner right around the anus. He stated that there was one small laceration, or one small cut, at the nine o'clock position, using the spine as 12 o'clock.

"Dr. McRae acknowledged, as did Dr. Markesteyn, that the skull fractures and the broken neck, coupled with the injuries to the anal area, were consistent with a sexual attack.

"And then you will recall again the testimony of the first police officer to arrive on the scene, Constable Steinthorson, as he described the position of the body, noting that the child was nude from the waist down. You observed in one of the photographs in Exhibit 3 that the little girl's panties were down around her feet.

"The nude lower body is but further demonstrable evidence of a sexual assault.

"Now, I have no doubt that my learned friend will have much to say about the fact that Mr. Bowman, the serologist who testified yesterday, found no evidence of seminal fluid or staining on the clothing of either the accused or the deceased. And indeed, the pelvic examination of the child revealed no evidence to suggest that sexual intercourse had taken place. But, ladies and gentlemen, the evidence establishes that it was during a sexual assault, which my lady, I know, will define for you, that death occurred. So I say to you that the non-existence of seminal staining is of no moment. There is ample and overwhelming evidence of sexual assault."

I proceeded to review the testimony of Ferlon Goosehead, Corrine Demas and others, which underscored the Crown's contention that James was not drunk or insane when he committed the sexual assault and murder.

"There isn't a shred of evidence," I told the jurors, "from any of the witnesses who were with the accused shortly before the child was killed, to suggest that the accused was intoxicated. Quite the contrary. John James was not intoxicated when he took little Ruby to the garage.

"The evidence, I submit, clearly demonstrates that the accused was sober and that he knew precisely where he was and what he was doing at the time that he killed his victim, and he must accept full responsibility for his actions.

"There is a presumption of sanity. John James is presumed to be sane and to have been sane at the time that he killed the child. There is no evidence before this court that John James isn't as sane as you or I. There is no evidence that he is mentally retarded or deficient. There is no evidence that he suffers from blackouts, physical infirmity or anything else."

After briefly describing James, I challenged the jury to look at the evidence and consider his record of lies.

"On Saturday, September 14th, at 7:10 p.m., former constable Derek Gove said to James:

"'Who were you with last night?'

"He replied: 'My sister Sharon.'

"Lie number one!

"Sharon James said that she had seen him at her cousin's place on Wellington around one o'clock on Friday afternoon, September 13th. She swore that she hadn't seen him at any time during the evening of Friday the 13th.

"Ms. Keyser, you may have noticed, did not cross-examine Sharon on this point. Sharon had spoken the truth.

"A short time later at the Public Safety Building, Sergeant Preisentanz asked the accused:

"'Do you know a girl Corrine Demas?'

"'From Roseau, yeah,' James replied. The sergeant then asked the accused:

"'Did you see her last night?'

"He replied:

"'No, I hear she went to Montreal to school.'

"Lie number two!

"Ferlon Goosehead, Ronald Schweid, Janet Greene, Eva Courchene and Corrine Demas herself confirmed that she was not away at school in Montreal, but that she was with the accused in the Maryland Hotel around 8 p.m. on Friday, September 13th.

"Mr. Kee specifically asked each of the aforementioned five witnesses whether any other person or persons joined them at their table or tables at the Maryland Hotel.

"They were unanimous; Eli Tacan was not there.

"In his written statement, the accused stated: 'Me, Ferlon and Corrine walked over to the Maryland. We sat down and we were getting ready to order and the waiter asked us for ID, started arguing with him, got up and sat at another table. Corrine got up and said she was going to the washroom. Eli Tacan came over and started to talk.'

"Lie number three! The most innovative, the most awesome lie ever manufactured; the insidious—yes, the insidious fingering of a decent family man and group home counsellor as a baby killer! But that's what the accused did. He fingered Eli Tacan....

"Let us consider the James version of the background events leading up to the confession of Eli Tacan in the words of the accused himself:

"'Eli Tacan came over to the table and started to talk. Then we told him we couldn't get served because we didn't have ID.

"'Ferlon got up and went to talk to his cousin. Me and Eli went to the washroom, smoked two joints, went back to the table where Ferlon was. So Eli told us, 'Come sit with us for a while; we'll order and give you guys some.'

"'We went and sat with Eli, had one, then he started to ask me about Corrine. She had left when she went to the washroom.

"'I gave Eli the address and told him the second floor.

"'Me and Ferlon stayed there and Eli left. That was only about 8:30. Then Ferlon and the two girls left. Ferlon went to the washroom. Then he, Eli, came back and he started to tell me about it. He said he saw a little girl walking up toward the third floor, he grabbed her and took off with her. He grabbed her and went to a garage two blocks away. He said the little girl was crying for her grandmother.

"'Then he just stopped and started telling a joke. Ferlon came back and we laughed. Then I said I was going to fuck off home now. Took a walk down to Sargent, took a Mountain bus, jumped on a bus and went home.'

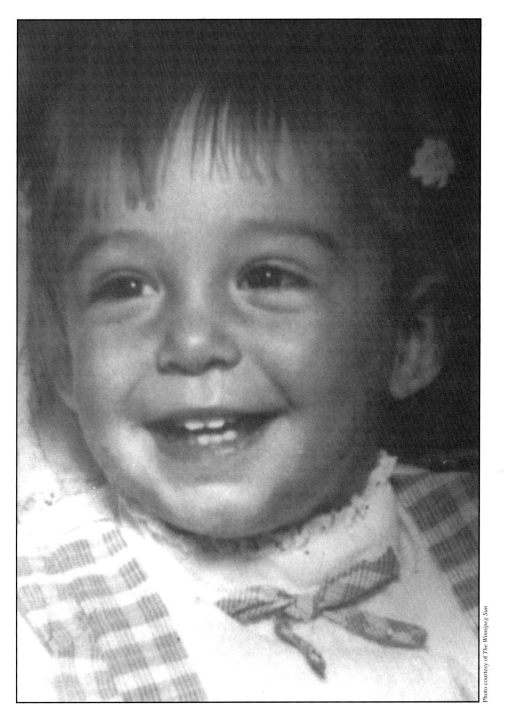

Ruby Adriaessens

John Thomas James Jr.

Kim Adriaessens

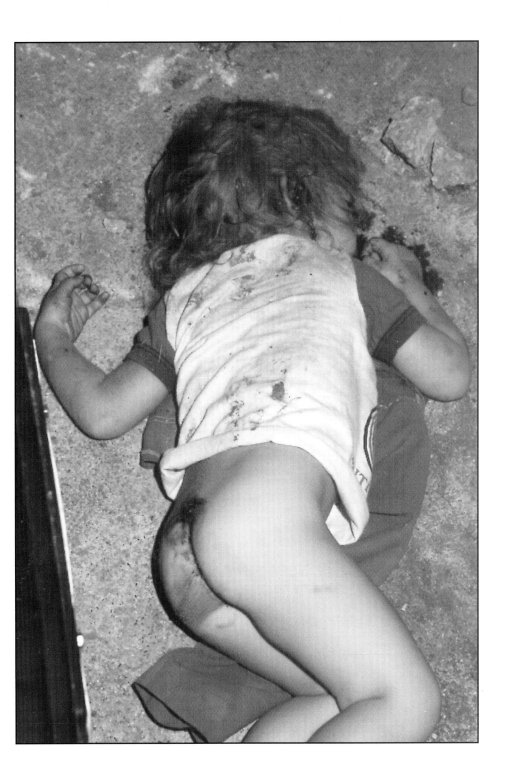

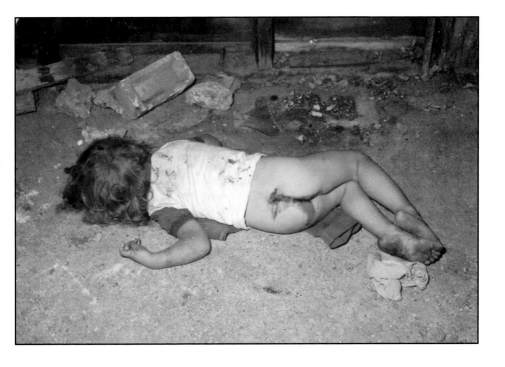

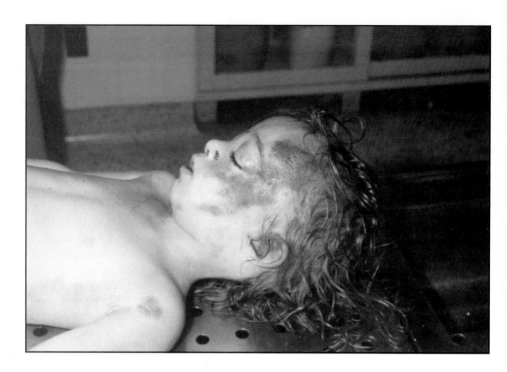

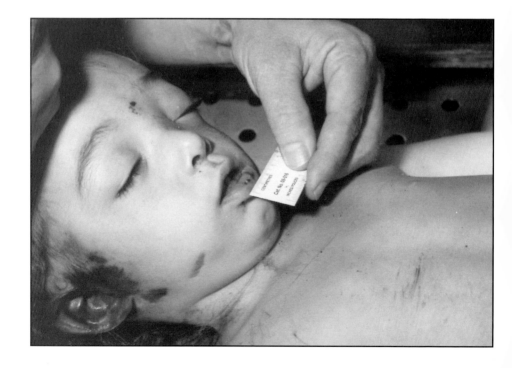

"Sergeant Preisentanz," I reminded the jury, "asked James how long he had known Eli.

"'About a year and a half,' he replied.

"'Can you describe him?' the sergeant asked.

"'He is about five feet, 11 inches; 160 pounds; he's wearing blue jeans; has zits on his face; he's about 23. He had a red Sioux Valley baseball jacket on with his name on the left side and "Third Base" on the right side,' James said."

I then reviewed in detail the testimony given by Tacan, a father, group home counsellor, amateur baseball and hockey player, and elected councillor of the Sioux Valley band.

Tacan had told the court that he worked from midnight to 8 a.m. on Friday/Saturday, September 13/14 at the Sioux Valley Group Home. His practice was to arrive at his job about half an hour early. He was not in Winnipeg on September 13, nor was he in the city on the 12th or 14th. He did not know the accused, except through media reports of the murder case, and he did not know any of the other five individuals included in the drinking party at the Maryland Hotel on September 13.

"In his oral and written statements," I noted, "the accused tells us precisely where he himself, not Eli Tacan, but where he himself grabbed the child—'The little girl was walking up to the third floor'....

"He tells you that the little girl was crying for her grandmother. Of course little Ruby was crying for her grandmother; she was shrieking in terror and crying for help.

"Shirley Adriaenssens went back up to Suite 9 on the third floor, you will recall, after having taken the bread out of the oven. She had gone down to her own suite, Suite 4, at about 8 p.m. She was babysitting Ruby. The child had accompanied her....

"The evidence is uncontradicted. Shirley Adriaenssens stayed in Suite 4 for five or 10 minutes.

"Tania testified that Ruby had stayed in Suite 4 for only a short time after her grandmother had left. She let Ruby out of the apartment because the child was too small to reach the door-knob.

"Tania thought she heard Ruby scream from the hallway.

"Yes, just as John James had said—'a little girl walking up toward the third floor.'

"He was the only one who knew the very place where the child had been snatched; he, who has the audacity to finger an innocent man, Eli Tacan."

The court took a short recess. I wandered out into the corridor, lit my pipe and strolled along the wide hallways, puffing and reflecting. So far, the jury had been attentive.

I thought about a paper I delivered years ago concerning trial tactics in criminal cases. I smiled as I remembered the opening paragraphs.

"As I stand before a jury, it is my practice to do two things before speaking. Firstly, I close my eyes and bow my head and offer a fervent, silent prayer for a conviction; and then, secondly, I remove my wristwatch and place it on the lectern. This latter manoeuvre is neither designed nor calculated to elicit a favourable response from the jury—'This lad means business. He will see to it that we don't sit about here all week.' No, I just want to record the time of the first fidget, or squirm or yawn. I've been keeping these statistics for years. Jury or audience reaction to my words has always intrigued me. I believe it was Lord Justice Chitty who had an ancient, tedious barrister before him, arguing at length about a bill of sale and the value of certain items including tables and chairs.

"'My lord,' the dreary old fool intoned, 'I now address myself to the furniture.'

"'You have been,' the jurist allowed caustically, 'for the past hour.'[1]

"Trial lawyers work in a world of words. Some induce fidgets and squirms and yawns more rapidly than others. Surely, as advocates, we must constantly strive to improve our forensic skills so that we address 12 alert, wide-eyed triers of the facts. All too frequently, I have addressed myself to the furniture."

Counsel were summoned to return to court. I deposited the white ash in one of the new cylindrical receptacles and hurried back with a commitment to cut it short. And yet, there was still so much to say, to emphasize, and to drive home.

I resumed my analysis of James's written statement.

"Eli Tacan," I began, "is alleged to have said that he took the little girl to a garage two blocks away.

"None of the police officers had told the accused where the little girl was found. The accused had volunteered this information.

"He told them precisely where he, not Eli Tacan, had taken Ruby Adriaenssens.

"A total stranger grabbed the child in her own apartment building. He took her to a darkened garage and started to violate her sexually.

"Of course she was crying for her grandmother. This is the one utterance in the accused's statement which I think you can find to be true.

"She screamed and cried out in her terror and pain. And during her hellish ordeal, the accused killed her.

"The garage was in a residential area. The police officers described the lighting conditions. Cumberland is a busy street. We know the time on that Friday night when the assault occurred.

"She screamed out and he stifled those screams or he would have been caught with the child in the darkened garage.

"Yes, she cried out for her grandmother.

"He had to stifle her screams—her plaintive cries for her grandmother, and—he killed her."

I paused, then walked to the exhibit table and picked up the booklet of photographs.

"I would ask you now to please look at Exhibit 12, the booklet containing the five photographs taken at autopsy.

"It is not my intention to try to inflame your passions or to arouse your sympathy when I ask you to do this."

I caught Drew Baragar, Keyser's able assistant, out of the corner of my eye. The young lawyer's face was wreathed in scepticism.

"You will recall Dr. Markesteyn having said that the pictures were very helpful to him in describing the child's injuries. He commented on the fact that these photographs were taken after the body had been washed.

"As you look at these photographs and recall the doctor's testimony, I suggest that three things will become even more abundantly clear: first of all, the nature and extent of the injuries sustained in this grotesquely sadistic assault; secondly, the degree of force required to fracture the skull, tear the brain and break the neck; and thirdly, the fact that the child's head came into contact with the cinder block which can be seen in photographs 7, 10 and 11."

The details were graphic indeed and were reinforced by my summation of Markesteyn's equally descriptive testimony of the injuries Ruby sustained. One juror held her hand over her mouth; others shuddered, their faces mirroring, in varying degrees, their anger, sorrow, sadness, outrage and pain.

I had been talking steadily for 15 minutes since the recess, but still had much ground to cover. I quickly turned to the police officers' testimony, re-emphasizing that no one viewed James as a suspect at the time he gave his written statement.

"Please recall Sergeant Anderson's testimony in this connection," I said. "He stated:

"'At five minutes past 11, Constable Gove and I re-entered Interview Room No. 1 with John James. I said, 'We're investigating the murder of a three-year-old girl last night. We've gone through your statement and what Goosehead told the police. It appears to us that you're lying about your knowledge of what happened last night. You've got to know more about what happened last night than what you're telling us. Why don't you tell us what really happened?'

"Sergeant Anderson stated that the accused looked down at the floor for approximately 10 seconds. Then he said:

"'I barely remember.'

"The sergeant then asked James: 'Do you remember anything at all about a little girl?'

"The accused replied:

"'Yeah. I grabbed her. I took her to a garage down the lane. Then I blacked out.'

"A clear, uncontradicted, voluntary admission right out of the accused's own mouth!

"The evidence is so overwhelming against the accused that I wonder if further comments from me are really necessary.

"Now, after James admitted to Sergeant Anderson and to Constable Gove that he had taken the little girl to the garage, James, the inveterate liar, added, as an afterthought:

"'I can't remember that well. I blacked out.'

"Is there any evidence before you of any physical illness on James's part? Any reason why he would have blacked out...? He was again reverting to his old lying self....

"You know, James is as poor a diagnostician as he is a liar.

"There is no evidence of drunkenness, no evidence of black-outs, but a great deal of uncontradicted evidence that the accused is a compulsive liar."

I focused next on the evidence that does not lie—the physical evidence presented mainly by James Cadieux of the R.C.M.P.

"Mr. Cadieux testified that he examined Exhibit 4, the large cinder block which was found in the garage at the rear of 695 Sherbrook Street in close proximity, as I have stressed, to the place where the body of the child was found. He testified that he examined a large clump of hair found on this block and, as well, one single hair, separate from the clump of hairs....

"[T]he single head hair found on the cinder block, separate from the large clump of hair, was consistent with the known hair sample from John James, the pulled hair sample.

"The scientist stated that, in examining the hair samples turned over to him, he magnified the hair approximately 125 to 150 times and was able to compare the properties of the hair; the cuticle, the cortex, and the medulla, if present, which comprises all hair.

"In viewing the cuticle, he told you, he observes the degree of serration, thickness, presence or absence of colour and the presence or absence of damage.

"In observing the cortex, he examines the overall colour, change of colour from root end to tip, and pigment granules as to size, shape and pattern of distribution; also, air vacuoles as to size, shape and pattern of distribution.

"In observing the medulla, the third component, he examines the pattern of distribution, thickness and opacity or translucency.

"He stated that the hair will vary from root end to tip. If the known hair and the questioned hair vary from root end to tip consistently, this is another criterion for finding the hairs consistent.

"He stated that there was no significant difference in any of these areas as between the single black scalp hair found on the cinder block and the scalp hair sample plucked from the head of John James.

"Mr. Cadieux stated, further, that the clump of hair found on the block was consistent with the hair pulled from Ruby Adriaenssens' head.

"He noted one further significant feature: damage or crushing of the proximal ends—that is, those closest to the scalp—which, he said, would be consistent with having been crushed by a blow with a blunt object.

"The scientist told you that he found 15 hairs on the white shroud used to cover the body of the deceased child. Five hairs were consistent with the pulled head hair from Ruby Adriaenssens.

"Four hairs were not consistent with any known hair sample. One scalp hair was consistent in all properties with the head hair of John James.

"On the brown paper bag used to cover Ruby's head, he found one scalp hair consistent in all properties with the head hair pulled from the accused, John James.

"Fifty hairs were visually consistent with Ruby's hair.

"On Exhibit 20, the men's white socks seized from the accused, he found one scalp hair, consistent in all properties with the hair pulled from Ruby's head. I ask you to recall that Mr. Cadieux told you that this hair included damage to the proximal end consistent with damage to the hair found on the cinder block in the large clump of hairs. He stated, you will remember, that this damage was consistent with a blow from a blunt object crushing the end of the hair.

"He examined the hairs and fibres in the vacuum bag, Exhibit 26. There he found one pubic hair, consistent in all properties with the pubic hairs plucked from John James.

"This pubic hair was found on the garage floor at the rear of 695 Sherbrook Street in the immediate area where Ruby's body was found.

"Recall, if you will, Sergeant Bellingham's testimony in this connection. He told you that, immediately after the body had been removed from the garage, and on two subsequent occasions, he vacuumed an area approximately six feet long and three feet wide to the right side of the cinder block as shown in Exhibit 3, photograph number 4.

"I pause here, ladies and gentlemen, to ask you to reflect upon how it came to pass that one of John James's pubic hairs was found in close proximity to the location where a semi-nude child was found.

"I know where I find the odd pubic hair: on the floor of my shower stall. But in a garage? What's that consistent with? It is consistent with all of the evidence we have heard about a sexual attack, and it is inconsistent with any other rational conclusion, I suggest.

"In the vacuum bag, Exhibit 14, containing hair and fibre collected from the garage floor, Mr. Cadieux found three scalp hairs, consistent in all properties with the hair from John James's head.

"On Exhibit 17, the black T-shirt worn by John James, he found one scalp hair consistent with the pulled hair from Ruby's head.

"The Crown respectfully suggests to you that the one scalp hair found on the cinder block, the three scalp hairs from the garage floor and the one pubic hair found on the garage floor, all found in close proximity to where Ruby's body was found, can lead to only one conclusion, one inalterable conclusion, one conclusion beyond all reasonable doubt whatsoever. John James was in that garage in that exact location with Ruby Adriaenssens.

"It is the Crown's contention that the scalp hairs, consistent with James's head hair found on the white shroud and the brown bag, both covering Ruby's body, coupled with the scalp hair found on the T-shirt and socks of the accused, lead to one conclusion, especially given the fact that the head hair on the sock worn by James was consistent with Ruby's head hair to the extent of being consistently damaged, as was Ruby's head hair found on the cinder block.

"Having regard, then, to all of these incredible matches, I say to you that there can be no doubt whatsoever but that John James was present in that garage at the rear of 695 Sherbrook Street with Ruby Adriaenssens on Friday night, the 13th of September, 1985.

"You will recall Mr. Cadieux's testimony with respect to the reliability or veracity of hair matches. And I want you to consider carefully what the young Mr. Cadieux said in this connection:

"'It is my experience and that of other experts that coincidental matches in human hair comparisons are relatively rare events. The chance that the questioned hair did indeed originate from the same source as the known sample is by far the more likely of the two possibilities.'

"And now we move on to a consideration of the fibres, if I may.

"Mr. Cadieux testified that one of his fields of scientific expertise is the comparison of cloth fibres.

"He told you that fibres are divided primarily into two groups: natural, such as wool and cotton, and synthetic, such as polyester and acrylic.

"He stated that the natural fibres such as cotton and wool can be compared as to their composition, their colour and their fluorescent properties.

"The synthetic materials, such as polyester and acrylics, he said, can be compared in relation to their colour, cross-sectional shape and width of fibre. Then he spoke about delustrants: their size, shape, pattern of distribution, dye and their fluorescent properties.

"He testified that he examined the black leather jacket, Exhibit 21, which was seized from the accused James. He observed that the black sleeve bands are composed of black polyester.

"He stated that he found fibres consistent in all properties in relation to the polyester fibres on Exhibit 6, Ruby's red overalls.

"He testified that he examined Exhibit 17, the black T-shirt seized from James, which was composed of black polyester and black cotton fibres.

"He found on the deceased's blue panties, her red overalls and on her T-shirt, and on the tape lifts from the child's body, one or more fibres which were consistent with the fibres which composed the accused's black T-shirt.

"He told you that the black sweatpants seized from the accused were composed of black polyester and cotton fibres and that fibres consistent with the fibres from the sweatpants were found on the child's red overalls.

"He testified that the black hat seized from John James was composed of wool and acrylic fibres.

"He stated that the fibre consistent with the known sample from this hat was consistent in all properties and was found on Ruby's overalls, white T-shirt and the tape lifts containing fibres from Ruby's body.

"Yes, even fibres from that hat he was seen wearing were found on the little child's overalls....

"Mr. Cadieux testified that polyester fabrics comprising the black T-shirt, sweatpants and black jacket seized from James were of different polyester types. He stated that the greater number of matches as between fibres, and with the inclusion of different types of fabrics—that is, three different types of polyester—the higher the degree of probability that the questioned fibres originated from and were consistent with the known samples.

"You will recall that Mr. Cadieux testified on cross-examination that there were no fibres from Ruby's clothes found on the clothes of John James.

"As well, you will recall a very astute question put by my lady to Mr. Cadieux in this respect in connection with the effect washing would have on the garments.

"Mr. Cadieux said that these fibres, if they had been present, would likely be lost or disappear if clothes were washed.

"And please recall that John James's second cousin, Harry James…told you that, on Saturday morning, September the 14th, John borrowed clothes from him while he, John James, washed his clothing.

"In concluding my remarks with respect to the hair and fibre evidence…let me say this to you. The totality of this evidence can lead only to certain inalterable conclusions:

"Firstly, that Ruby Adriaenssens did not have a mere casual connection with John James at some place other than the garage on Friday the 13th; and secondly, given the large number of hair and fibre matches and where they were found, on the accused's clothing, on the deceased child's clothing, on her naked skin, on the garage floor in the immediate area where the body was found, on the cinder block in close proximity to the body, coupled with the fact that she died almost instantaneously, the conclusion is inalterable.

"The conclusion, the only rational conclusion, I respectfully urge, is that John James and Ruby Adriaenssens were together in that garage at the rear of 695 Sherbrook Street when she died….

"I am sure that my learned friend will have something to say to you about the fact that the accused's blue jeans and runners weren't tendered in evidence. She may also question why the Crown had failed to produce many more exhibits….

"The blue jeans and the runners have absolutely no probative value. They would have afforded no legal proof of anything whatsoever. They wouldn't have taken us two inches beyond the line of scrimmage. That is why they weren't tendered in evidence."

The incessant pacing and moving had ceased. The aggressiveness was gone. I spoke very softly. I was placid.

"There may be some of you who will feel a degree of sympathy for John James because, I think it is fair to say, that life hasn't smiled sweetly upon him.

"And I think there would be a natural tendency and inclination to feel anguish in your hearts for the mother and the sister and the grandmother and the aunt and the uncle of little Ruby.

"Maybe you can cast your mind back to that Monday morning in eternity, or was it just a week and a half ago, when each and every one of you held the Holy Bible in your hand and took your oath as juror: 'You shall well and truly try and true deliverance make between our Sovereign Lady the Queen and the prisoner at the bar, whom you shall have in charge, and a true verdict give, according to the evidence.'

"'According to the evidence' takes into account neither revulsion nor sympathy.

"'A true verdict, according to the evidence.'

"I respectfully say to you...that when you consider in their totality all of the undisputed, uncontradicted, proven facts, you will come to the conclusion that John Thomas James Jr. committed murder in the first degree upon the person of Ruby Adriaenssens; that he murdered her.

"And I respectfully suggest to you that the evidence is inconsistent with any other rational conclusion; no other rational conclusion than that the accused is guilty as charged.

"I want to conclude by saying this to you...that long after my friend, Ms. Keyser, is no longer around to defend those who are charged with crime, and long after Mr. Kee and I have left the office of the Crown prosecutor, the admonition from Holy Writ which was the law of our fathers' fathers shall still be the law of our children's children—Thou Shalt Not Kill!

"As this solemn inquiry into the truth draws gradually to a close, ladies and gentlemen, I ask you for one thing, nothing more and nothing less—a true verdict, according to the evidence."

CHAPTER **11**

The Address for the Defence

Her obligatory preliminary comments completed, Brenda Keyser spoke directly to the jurors.

"For the past week and a half, you have all been participants in the jury system of justice. And that is a system where the 12 of you have been chosen to decide the facts in this case. Only you can do that. My lady will instruct you on the law and you are bound to follow those instructions, but you alone will render the verdict based on the facts that you decide.

"You have been participating in a democratic system of justice where the guilt or innocence of an accused person is decided on the basis of the evidence presented in court during a trial and on nothing else.

"Now, before you were selected as jurors in this trial, you heard my lady put a question to each and every one of you individually. And the question was whether or not you would be able to put aside anything you might have heard or read in the media, any preconceived ideas that you might have had before you were chosen to sit on this jury and render a verdict only on the evidence that you have heard in this past week and a half.

"Now it is unusual to put a question like that to jury members. And it was done because this has become such an emotional case. And when we look back at the evidence that we have heard in the past week and a half, it would be hard not to be moved by the evidence; the evidence outlined by Dr. Markesteyn on the stand, the little girl's injuries as outlined by my learned friend in such graphic detail for you. You saw the family of Ruby Adriaenssens and no doubt you can feel what they must feel.

"But, as jurors, and as the sole triers of the facts in this case, you cannot rely on sympathy. And that means you must put aside sympathy for the death of a three-year-old child. You must put aside sympathy for the plight of a 17-year-old boy on trial for her murder. And these emotions, difficult as it may be, must be left outside the jury room when you go inside to begin your deliberations.

"You must consider each and every fact that has been brought forward and placed before you during the course of this trial. And, like my learned friend, I watched you closely during the trial and I know all of you paid extreme attention to the evidence that was presented. You and you alone must decide what facts to pick out of that mass of evidence that you heard, which ones to accept and which ones to reject.

"It's not up to the police to tell you that an individual is guilty. If that were the case, we wouldn't need juries and we wouldn't need judges. And I caution you, when you are beginning your deliberations, the evidence of a police officer is worth no more than the evidence of any other witness that you have heard."

The comment angered Kee, normally a man of self-restraint.

"She ought to know: she's married to an ex-cop," he whispered.

Keyser went on:

"You are just as free to reject that evidence and accept the evidence of another witness. It's not up to the newspapers or the media to decide whether an accused is guilty or not guilty. It's not up to the Crown prosecutor, it's not even up to her ladyship to render a verdict in this matter, it's up to you 12.

"Now, one of the cornerstones of our judicial system is the presumption of innocence. It's very, very important. When John James Jr. walked into this courtroom a week and a half ago, he was innocent. And, even as he sits here this afternoon in that box, he is innocent. He is innocent until each and every one of you 12 decide otherwise. You are going to hear a lot about that. You heard a lot about it from my learned friend. You are going to be hearing a lot about it from me. And you are going to be hearing a lot about it from my lady. And along with this presumption of innocence is the notion that, at all times, it's the Crown that must prove the guilt of an accused beyond this reasonable doubt. John James Jr. doesn't have to come here and try to convince you that he is not guilty. It's not the way our system works. He is innocent. The Crown must prove him guilty, guilty beyond any reasonable doubt; guilty in the eyes of all 12 of you, individually, beyond a reasonable doubt.

"My lady will later instruct you on the law and I am sure that she will be telling you that if you are not satisfied on any issue, beyond a reasonable doubt, that it's your duty, it's your obligation, based on the oath you took, to resolve that doubt in the favour of John James Jr. That is the law and you are bound to follow it.

"And bear in mind when you consider that, that John James Jr. is entitled to sit mute in that box and say to the Crown, 'You are alleging that I did something. Prove it, and prove it to the degree that is necessary in our judicial system.'

"Now, the case that you have heard put before you over the past week and a half is like a jigsaw puzzle. You have to put the pieces together. Bear in mind that there is not a single witness that saw John James Jr. with Ruby Adriaenssens in the block or on the way to the garage. There is not a single witness who has come forward who said that he saw John James Jr. with Ruby Adriaenssens, crossing busy Cumberland Avenue on the way to the garage.

"Now the evidence is like bits and pieces that have to come together. And the Crown suggests to you this morning that the pieces fit together in only one way, and that that way proves beyond a reasonable doubt, and it's ludicrous to suggest otherwise, that John James Jr. is guilty of murder."

Would I ever live long enough, I wondered wearily, to be involved in a circumstantial case where no one dug up that old, worn-out jigsaw puzzle analogy?

"The Crown would have you believe," Keyser said with a tinge of indignation, "that John James grabbed a three-year-old child and took her to a garage some distance away where he sexually assaulted and killed her; even bought himself a Slurpee and went off to meet his friend, Eileen McKinney.

"Now, let's examine the theory of the Crown in light of all of the evidence that you have heard over the last week and a half. And let's look particularly at the pieces of evidence that the Crown relies on in its theory.

"Opportunity to commit the murder? The Crown has suggested to you that, after leaving the Maryland, John James returned to the block on Notre Dame, presumably to see Corrine Demas, and, instead, grabbed a three-year-old child.

"Now, you heard the evidence of Shirley Adriaenssens, the grandmother of the little girl, who is babysitting up at Ruby's apartment that evening. She testified on the stand that she went down to her apartment about eight o'clock that night. And she knows that, because she had bread in the oven. So we can rely on her time with a fair amount of certainty. She is there for five or 10 minutes and then she leaves Ruby in the care of her younger daughter, Tania, and returns up to Ruby's apartment.

"Tania came and testified that Ruby didn't stay very long in the apartment. She left after a few minutes. Tania had to help her open the door. It would seem that Ruby left the apartment about a quarter after eight on the evening of September 13th, 1985. Tania testified, as well, that she thought she heard some screams right away. And we know that Ruby never made it upstairs to her own apartment. It's only one flight of stairs. And even for a small child, that would take a few minutes at most to go from the second to the third floor. So I think it is reasonable for you to assume that, within a few minutes of leaving the suite that Tania was in, that Ruby went missing.

"Where was John James at 8:15? One of the last Crown witnesses you heard was Corrine Demas. Corrine hadn't been drinking that night, not during any of her contact with John. She testified that she went to Debbie Gouvreau's suite in the same block where the little girl was about eight o'clock that night.

She testified that she was there for 10 minutes, or so, and then she walked to the Maryland with John James and with Ferlon Goosehead. It takes about five minutes to walk to the Maryland. So at 8:15, John James is either walking to the Maryland Hotel with Ferlon Goosehead and Corrine Demas, two of the Crown's witnesses, or he is at the Maryland trying to get served.

"Is there any other evidence that backs that up? Well, look at what Ferlon Goosehead said. Ferlon estimated that John left the Maryland Hotel between 8:30 and 8:45 that Friday evening. In other words, he didn't leave the Maryland Hotel until 15 to 30 minutes after the little girl went missing. And John told Ferlon that he was heading home. If he was going back to that block to try and find Corrine, why wouldn't he have told Ferlon that when he left the Maryland Hotel? He had no reason not to tell Ferlon that."

A juror in the second row frowned and shook his head from side to side. All counsel, at one time or another during such a trial, glance furtively at the faces of the jury, searching for an omen—good or ill.

"These are Crown witnesses and witnesses who have no relation to John. They have no reason to lie. They're not covering up for him.

"Has the Crown proven to your satisfaction that John had the opportunity to commit that murder? And I ask you to think about that very carefully because that is one of the pieces in the puzzle that the Crown relies on.

"The Crown has theorized that, because nobody saw this, John took Ruby Adriaenssens to the garage where her body was found some distance away—in the early evening hours of September 13th, walking with a three-year-old girl—having to cross Cumberland Avenue—and you heard Constable Boan testifying that Cumberland is a busy street. Now, to get from Notre Dame to that garage, you have to cross that busy street, and in the early evening hours of a Friday night near the Maryland Hotel, not one person saw or heard anything. And you heard that a search was launched right after the little girl was found missing. Not one person has come forward to say that they saw anything.

"Now, even at that time, if you didn't realize it, don't you think that once you heard about the murder of a little girl that you would remember seeing a dark-haired Indian boy dragging a screaming blonde child some distance away from her home? That is something you would notice and it would jar your consciousness because it's not a young Native boy walking with a young Native girl that might be his own daughter, that might be his younger sister. This is something you would remember, you would notice. It's not the middle of the night. You are not in a deserted part of the country. And the Crown has told you that the little girl was crying and screaming for her grandmother. How is it that nobody heard that?"

Keyser took a sip of water and pressed on.

"What is the next piece of evidence that the Crown asks you to rely on? The lies of John James himself. Well, let's look at those lies. Let's examine firstly the testimony of Sharon James and Eileen McKinney. And these are very important witnesses because these are the first people that John talked to about where he had been the previous night. This is before he knew he was suspected of doing anything. What does he tell them both? Well, he tells them both that he went drinking, which we know is true. He sees Eileen McKinney, by her estimation, at 9:30 that Friday night. Seems normal to her. And she knows him. He has been staying at the same residence. He is not worried or sweating; he is calm; he is sipping a Slurpee. Does that sound to you like someone who has just sexually molested and bludgeoned to death a three-year-old girl? And if he had done that, and was talking to Eileen to set up an alibi, he wouldn't pick one that was so easily disproved.

"And we know that he has feelings. We know that that is not the reason he was calm when he met Eileen, because he gets upset when he is at the police station and he starts to cry at one point when he is being questioned by the police officers. He has emotions.

"So that is not the explanation for why he is calm. I ask you to think about that very seriously.

"Now, he talks to Eileen that night and he appears calm in

every respect. Next morning he talks to his sister Sharon. He trusts her. He has no reason not to. What does he tell his sister? Well, he tells his sister that he went drinking with Ferlon Goosehead and Corrine Demas, which we know is true. He tells her, as well, that he met Eileen McKinney, which we know is true. And he tells her that, between going drinking with Ferlon Goosehead and Corrine Demas and meeting up with Eileen McKinney, that he went to his cousin Stan's on Burrows. Now he also tells the sister that he went there with Corrine and we know that is not true.

"The Crown says to you," Ms. Keyser scoffed, "read into that, read into that lie, translate that lie into guilty of murder. But look at that. Look at it closely. And is that the only reason that a 17-year-old boy would lie about being with a girl that he wasn't with? Now if he really needed an alibi for what went on that Friday night, why would he say he went with Corrine when it's so easily disproved? He says he went to Stan's on Burrows. Now that is a perfect alibi if he needs an alibi. 'I went to Stan's and no one was home.' Why lie about Corrine Demas? Why tell Sharon that he was with Corrine when Corrine ties him right back to the block where the little girl was missing? Doesn't make sense.

"Now if it wasn't to cover up for a murder, was there another explanation as to why he would lie to the sister about that? This is a 17-year-old kid and we know from the testimony of Ferlon Goosehead and Corrine Demas that John is interested in Corrine. He wanted to go out with her. And, in Corrine's vocabulary, he was 'coming on' to her that Friday evening and she rebuffed him because she had other plans and she didn't want to be bothered. So he tells his big sister that he was with Corrine that night. He tells her that what he wanted to happen actually happened. That is the wishful thinking of a teenager. There is a more plausible explanation why he is lying to his sister about that small point. Certainly makes a poor alibi, but it's a good story to impress your sister that you have been out with the girl you wanted to go out with.

"And I ask you to consider carefully, has the Crown satisfied

114

you to that degree necessary, beyond a reasonable doubt, that John didn't go to Stan's as he said? With Corrine, no, we know he didn't go with Corrine. But have they satisfied you that he didn't go there? John told them he had been there. Stan wasn't called. It's not up to John to prove that he was there. The burden of proof is always on the Crown.

"Now Saturday morning what happens? Harry James finds John asleep in a chair. He is still dressed. What is he wearing? He is wearing the same clothes he had on Friday morning when Harry saw him, Friday evening when Eileen saw him. What were those clothes? Jeans and a grey T-shirt that you saw here this week. This is not his second cousin trying to help him out of a jam. This is the same thing Corrine Demas saw him wearing, the grey T-shirt. And she identified that grey T-shirt, as well as Harry James.

"And I ask you to remember that, because it's important. It's important for other reasons that I will touch on later on in my submission.

"And bear in mind as well that Corrine has no reason to lie. She is not a close friend of John's. Far from it. She has rebuffed his attentions.

"What does Harry James say about what John is like on Saturday morning? He is not upset, he is perfectly normal, just like Ferlon Goosehead said about John's attitude when he left the Maryland Hotel. He wasn't angry or upset. Just like Eileen McKinney said when she saw him at 9:30 that night. He is not sweating, he is not nervous, he is not panicky.

"Now later on...I am going to be telling you that, often, what you don't hear about, or what isn't put before you, is as important as what is put before you. And, in this context, what John James doesn't do is as important as what he does do. What he doesn't do is flee.

"You heard testimony that he was from Roseau River. He still had family down there. His father lived on the reserve. If he had just brutally murdered a young child the night before, don't you think he'd be on a bus to Roseau River that day?

"Police come to 89 Lorne Avenue where John is staying with

Harry about 7 p.m. And they ask him to go with them to the Public Safety Building. He agrees without hesitation.

"Now, the Crown would have you believe that the testimony of the police officers is really all you need to convict John James. Well, it's not that clear-cut and I ask you to look at the evidence of the police as carefully as you look at the evidence of the other witnesses. And when you are doing that, bear in mind that talking to a police officer is not like talking to a friend, it's not like talking to Eileen McKinney, it's not like talking to your big sister. The police can be intimidating even without meaning to be because they are authority figures.

"How many of you have had a police cruiser pull up behind your car? You feel uncomfortable even though you know you haven't done anything because you think the police might think you have done something wrong. Otherwise, why would they be stopping you? It's a natural reaction when people deal with the police. It's because they're powerful authority figures. And how much more so for a 17-year-old Native boy in an interview room at the Public Safety Building?

"And you heard a description of the room that he was kept in for so long. It's a small room, tile floor, table, some wooden chairs without arms, no windows in the room, door closed. And for that four-hour period, John is either in that room with two big police officers or he is left alone in there with the door closed to think, to stew, to wonder. And I say to you…that that is an intense, intimidating place for a 17-year-old boy to be.

"Now, Sergeant Preisentanz and Mr. Gove went in first to deal with John. They're the first police officers that had dealings with him. And you saw them both testify. You saw the size of both of them. Sergeant Preisentanz is six feet, three inches, 230 pounds. He outweighs John by a hundred pounds himself, let alone Mr. Gove in the room as well. Neither of them can help being big, but consider how intimidating that is for a 17-year-old boy. People that big, two of them, in a small room asking for you to account for your whereabouts the previous night.

"And bear in mind that he doesn't even know why he is there because they haven't told him. They haven't told him he is just a witness and all they want is information. He doesn't know why he is there. And I put it to you...that anybody in the position of John James that evening would reasonably think that they were being suspected of doing something wrong by the questions that were being asked—'Where were you? Who were you with? What were you wearing?' Without being told why he is being asked those questions. Now even if in reality he wasn't a suspect, and the police say he wasn't, the police haven't told him that. He doesn't know he is not a suspect.

"Now John tries to be co-operative with the police. He tells them where he was the night before, and basically tells them the truth."

It is basic statements like this containing basic half-truths, I reflected sorrowfully, that make people basically mistrust most lawyers.

"His basic whereabouts," Keyser pointed out, "are verified by other Crown witnesses. What does he leave out? He leaves out being at the block, 628 1/2 Notre Dame, and he leaves out being with Corrine Demas. That is what he doesn't tell the police at first. And the Crown says to you, 'He is lying, and that should make you suspicious of John James.' The police say it doesn't make them suspicious of him, so why should it make you suspicious of him?

"But why wouldn't he admit to the police that he had been at the block and that he had been with Corrine? There must have been something on his mind for him not to have told them about that. Well, we know from what Corrine said and what Ferlon said that John had been 'coming on to her,' to use her terms, the previous day. And he wanted to go out with her. He has got her on his mind to the extent that he mentions her to his big sister.

"Now, I put it to you...that this is some time after that little girl went missing. If he was guilty, he had a lot of time to think of a much better story than what he was coming out with at this point. But what is going on in his mind other than being guilty of murder? Why doesn't he mention being at the block and why doesn't he mention being with Corrine? Put yourself in John James's position—'I was coming on to Corrine last night. Did she make a complaint to the police about me? Is that why I'm here?' He doesn't know because he hasn't been told. And, later on, the police put specific questions to him about that block and about Corrine. And this time he denies it—'I wasn't there. It wasn't me, man.' The police are interested in Corrine. Clearly, that is uppermost in his mind by the responses to his questions; otherwise, why would he avoid mentioning Corrine Demas when he has already told the police he was with Ferlon Goosehead? It doesn't make any sense.

"Now, at one point he even says to the two officers in the room, 'Look, am I being charged with something?' He is bewildered. He doesn't know why he is there. They still haven't told him. Is he reassured by the police? Is he told, 'No, we're not here about Corrine, we're here about a specific investigation. We think you can help us.' He is not told. They brush off his concerns. They don't address him. They continue asking him questions.

"It is sometime during the second interview when he has been in this room with these two police officers for some period of time that they finally tell him that a little girl from that block was killed the night before. Now, before he even has a chance to answer that question, the partner of that police officer, Mr. Gove, is asking John James if he knows about a polygraph, if he knows what a polygraph is. Well, what is a reasonable person to conclude out of a question like that? 'Why are you police asking me about a polygraph unless you think I am lying?' Now he knows why they're there. It's clear from his answers to those questions— 'Shit, man, I'm into B and E's, not this.' It's clear from that response that he thinks the police think he killed that little girl. Whether they did or not, it's clear from his answer…that that is what is in his mind. And you can see that from the answer he gave to the police.

"And consider the police officers. They're a little hepped up. They have to be. This is a serious investigation. This is a very serious crime. It's important to them to find out who is responsible. And that is why they're pressing John. They're not letting up. They're going to continue questioning him. We're not talking about a shoplifting case where they're going to give you a cursory list of questions and let you be on your way. They're going to press. They're going to find out. And that is the atmosphere in that small interview room in the Public Safety Building with that 17-year-old boy.

"Now, half-way through this interview when John is finally told why he is there, he realizes this is serious. It's a murder they're talking about. And he realizes now that he is not there for anything that has to do with Corrine Demas. And he admits being at the block at 628 1/2 Notre Dame and he admits being with Corrine Demas. Now he knows that is not a concern to the police.

"He then tells the police about Eli Tacan. My learned friend says, 'Why would he point the finger at an innocent man if he is not guilty and trying to cover his tracks?' Well, why would he tell the police about Eli Tacan if he is not guilty? He thought he was being accused of murder. Anybody would, in his shoes, by the questions being put to him. And he invents a story that is not rational, it's not logical, it's not mature, it's not even very bright. But you're talking about an immature person who finds himself in an irrational place, irrational setting. And why tell such a story that is so easily torn apart, that can be so easily checked? The descriptions, the addresses, the whereabouts of Mr. Tacan can all be so easily disproved. And he has had lots of time, if he wanted an alibi, to think of a better one than that.

"Why not give them a vague story about hitting the bars on Main Street and drinking with people he didn't know before going to see Eileen McKinney? It's an alibi and it can't be checked.

"Is it surprising, ladies and gentlemen of the jury, that a 17-year-old Native boy who thinks the police suspect him of murder would be worried that the police wouldn't believe him? They have already asked him about a polygraph and he knows that he has already lied to them about Corrine Demas. But bear in mind that he is not on trial for lying to the police. He is on trial for murder. And that is what has to be proven beyond a reasonable doubt.

"John James is scared. There is a big, burly police officer sitting a few feet away from him, telling him, finally, about the murder of a little girl, with his partner sitting a few feet away telling him about a polygraph, asking him about a polygraph. What kind of pressure is that for a 17-year-old kid? And I put it to you…that a person can lie out of fear, just as much as out of guilt. And I ask you to bear that in mind.

"Now, later on in the interview, John breaks down and cries. He is afraid and he cries. Does it seem reasonable to you that he is apparently more upset at being accused of murder than actually doing it? Because we know he was normal when he saw Eileen McKinney at 9:30 that Friday night. Think about that when you deliberate.

"The last thing he says before the police take a written statement from him was 'I wasn't there.' He is emotional and upset. You take a written statement from him and he wants to be out of there. He feels he is being accused of murder. He is like a frightened rabbit at this point….

"The police leave him alone in that room for a while, the sterile room where he has been sitting for almost four hours. His uncle isn't there. No adults are there with him. And after he is left there for a while, two new police officers come into the room—Sergeant Anderson and Constable Osborne. And both of them are slightly bigger than John is. And look at what is said to John. They tell him they think he is lying. Look at the words they used—'You've got to know more than what you are telling us. Why don't you tell us what really happened?'

"Those are the words of compulsion, ladies and gentlemen, words of commands. In his mind, that is as much as telling him they think he is guilty. And I ask you to consider, to a 17-year-old, are those requests for information or are those demands? And what is his response? He knows what they want to hear. He stares down at the floor for a long time and, in a quiet voice, says, 'I barely remember.' They keep on. 'What do you remember?' Again, in a quiet voice—'I grabbed her.' That is what the police wanted to hear. John James wants out. He wants an end to the questioning so he tells the police what they want to hear and it works.

"They say to him," counsel reminded the jurors, "'Do you want your uncle here?' 'Yes,' John replies. And they go and they get his uncle."

I glanced at my younger, agitated associate and thought, repressing an urge to smile, that he was feeling for all the maligned cops in Christendom.

Keyser continued, using a now all-too-familiar question:

"Are you satisfied, beyond a reasonable doubt, that what he told the police is the truth? Are you satisfied beyond a reasonable doubt?

"He tells the police that he knows about the little girl—this is later on in the interview—he says Eileen told him. That is how he knew about the little girl. The Crown called her as a witness and didn't ask her if that was a lie. And that comment to the police doesn't wipe out the rest of the evidence. It doesn't change the fact that, at 8:15, when Ruby went missing, John James was on his way to the Maryland Hotel or was at the Maryland Hotel. It doesn't change the testimony of Eileen McKinney as to his mood at 9:30 that Friday night. And it doesn't change the testimony of Corrine Demas as to his mood that evening. He wasn't upset. It doesn't change the testimony of Ferlon Goosehead as to his mood when he left the Maryland Hotel. And I ask you, ladies and gentlemen, to consider if that last statement to the police is true or just another story."

Keyser turned to the hair and fibre evidence presented by James Cadieux.

"He told us that hair analysis is not like fingerprints. You can't say that came from John James, that came from Ruby Adriaenssens, like fingerprints. I suggest that my learned friend would have you believe that it's that strong. But Mr. Cadieux admitted that it's not like fingerprints. The best you can say is that a hair or fibre is consistent with coming from a certain source. So it's not an exact science.

"Now, I read a passage, during my cross-examination, to Mr. Cadieux, a passage in an article written by a Mr. Gaudette who, Mr. Cadieux admitted, was an R.C.M.P. expert like himself.

Mr. Gaudette is a published author on the subject. Mr. Cadieux is familiar with his works. Mr. Cadieux said that he was familiar with the particular article in *The Journal of Forensic Sciences* that I referred him to. And what was the passage that I read to Mr. Cadieux? I'd like to read it to you again. I'd like you to think about it.

"'In the literature, there is considerable disagreement as to the value of hair evidence. In general, a disparaging view of hair examination has been taken.'

"Now, Mr. Cadieux admitted that that was the state of the literature, that there was this disagreement over the value of hair evidence. He, himself, did not subscribe to it, but he admitted that that was the state of the literature on the subject.

"Now, personally he feels that hair evidence is more valuable. It's not surprising that he wants his evidence to be accepted, to have some weight. And I am not suggesting by that that he is trying to make more of it than is there.

"On cross-examination, Mr. Cadieux revealed that John James has what is known as 'Mongoloid hair.' And that is hair that is common to Orientals and Native American Indians. And what is the significance of having 'Mongoloid hair'? There is less variety in the hair of people with Mongoloid hair and thus more chance of similarities between different people.

"Think about that, please, when you are assessing this evidence.

"Mr. Cadieux told us about the tests that he ran, and I don't profess to understand any of them. But I suggest that they raise some serious questions that you have to consider. Mr. Cadieux said that he found hairs that were consistent with having come from John James. Where?—the cinder block, paper bag, shroud, and the garage floor, the sample from the garage floor in the vial.

"Where did those hairs come from? Every one of those exhibits had contact with the garage floor. The cinder block was on the garage floor. The paper bag was on the garage floor when the head was put into it. The shroud had contact with the floor. The vial had scrapings from the floor. As well, consider that the shroud had nine hairs on it that couldn't have come from either John James or Ruby Adriaenssens. Because even if often you can't—or even if you can't say that a hair comes from a specific person, you can use it to eliminate it from coming from a person. Those nine hairs that couldn't have come from John James or Ruby Adriaenssens on the shroud, where did they come from? Last, has the Crown satisfied you that they didn't come from the person responsible?

"Now I mentioned to you earlier that often what you don't find is as important as what you do find. Maybe more so, in some cases. Now Dr. Markesteyn outlined injuries that were consistent with a struggle taking place. And we heard of hair being found clutched in the hands of the little girl, found in the mouth of the little girl. Now I ask each one of you, which is more likely to have come from the killer, hair from the garage floor or hair from the hands of a struggling child? Whose hair was it? We don't know. Where did it go? We don't know.

"And I ask you to look at what else is not there. There is not one hair consistent with coming from John James found on any of the clothing of Ruby Adriaenssens. Not one out of 51 hairs was found on her clothes. Not one hair consistent with coming from John James is found on her body tapings. Not one. And the Crown made much of the fact that some material wasn't found on John James's clothing because it was washed, presumably. And if there was this struggle, why is there not hair consistent with John James found on that clothing or those body tapings, if he in fact is the killer?

"Now, Mr. Cadieux said that he found hair consistent with coming from Ruby Adriaenssens on the pair of socks and the black T-shirt of John James. And all he can say, the best he can say is that it's consistent with coming from Ruby. Can't say it came from her. But what is more important is there is nothing, no hair that could have come from Ruby Adriaenssens found on the jacket of John, no hair from Ruby found on the sweatpants, found on the cap, found on the underwear, the grey T-shirt or the jeans of John James. And they all can't be explained by washing. You can't wash a leather jacket. Why isn't there something on the leather jacket? You don't wash a felt cap. Why isn't there something on the cap?

"Now, Mr. Cadieux said, as well, that he found hair consistent with coming from Ruby Adriaenssens on the black T-shirt, the one that two people have told us that John James was not wearing that night. That may be indicative of just how inexact the science of hair analysis is.

"Mr. Cadieux told us, as well, about fibres. And he said it's easier to find similarities with rare fibres. And we're not dealing here with rare fibres. We're dealing here with two natural fibres—wool, cotton—and a common synthetic, polyester. Those are the three fibres—three types of fibres he found. They're all common fibres.

"Now, Mr. Cadieux examined the clothing of Ruby Adriaenssens. Coveralls, the T-shirt and her body tapings have fibres which he says are consistent with having come from the cap of John James. And Mr. Cadieux talked about black fibres that make up this cap. Is that a black cap? It's a blue cap. You don't need a microscope to tell you that is a blue cap. And not one fibre from Ruby Adriaenssens' clothing, not one fibre consistent with having come from any of her clothing was found on that cap. And yet Mr. Cadieux tells us we should expect this transfer of fibres if there is contact. Not always, but it's a reasonable assumption that they're going to transfer. And you don't wash a felt cap, so that is not the explanation.

"In any event, remember back to what Eileen McKinney said. It's not the cap he was wearing that night. May have been one like it, but it wasn't that cap. And she is sure. And she is not lying to protect John James, because she doesn't say that it's not the jacket he was wearing. She positively identifies that leather jacket. She is just a very intuitive person. She notices things. How does she remember the jacket John had on that night? Paint specks on it. That is how she is able to say, 'I am very sure that is the jacket he had on.' And she very specifically said it's something like that cap, but it was definitely not that cap because it was a black cap, not a blue cap.

"Some of Ruby's clothing had fibres on it that Mr. Cadieux

says are consistent with having come from the black T-shirt that has been introduced into evidence, the black T-shirt of John James. There are no fibres from her clothes on that black T-shirt. It's hardly surprising because, according to Harry James, according to Corrine Demas, he wasn't wearing that black T-shirt. He had on his grey T-shirt that night. There is nothing in Ruby Adriaenssens' clothing that could have come from that grey T-shirt; no hairs or fibres.

"Now, Mr. Cadieux says, as well, that Ruby Adriaenssens' clothes have fibres that are consistent with having come from the cuffs of the leather jacket. But, again, where is the transfer of fibres? There are no fibres on the jacket consistent with coming from Ruby's clothing. Again, you don't wash a leather jacket, so that is not the explanation. That is not why those fibres aren't there. What about other fibres found in the area and on the little girl? Do we know where they all come from? No.

"Ladies and gentlemen of the jury, my learned friend has suggested to you that John James is guilty beyond a reasonable doubt because of the accumulation of probabilities. And I say to you that we don't have that here at all. Rather, what we have is an accumulation of improbabilities that don't add up.

"The decision that you are being asked to make here is an important one. It has very serious consequences. There is no more serious charge in the Criminal Code of Canada than that of first degree murder. And you will soon be called upon to decide a boy's entire future. The responsibility is so awesome that it leaves no room for error on your part.

"It's always tragic when a life is lost, particularly a young life. But, as horrible as the crime might be that you have heard outlined here to you this past week and a half, there is only one thing more horrible, and that is convicting an innocent boy.

"My lady will explain to you that the verdict you render must be the verdict of all 12 of you. If any one of you has any reasonable doubt, you have a duty to hang onto that doubt as if it were your last breath.

"And I ask you to give John James the same careful consideration that you would give a member of your own family.

"You swore under oath that you would give John James the benefit of any reasonable doubt. I trust that you will do your duty, remembering the promise you made."

CHAPTER 12

The Charge to the Jury

Lawyers who practise in the criminal courts are not very humble or self-effacing people as a rule.

I had watched them during the short-lived euphoria of court-room triumphs, accepting, unreservedly, the plaudits of their clients, claques and associates. Yet, never could I recall having heard a victorious counsel generously acknowledging the invaluable contribution of the trial judge who had charged the jury with masterful insight, clarity and objectivity.

I had watched them, as well, in the anguish of their defeat. And, as their shackled clients were towed from the courtroom by the all-too-smug sheriff's officers, I had listened to the lamentations of sombre counsel and to the venomous outbursts of the acid-tongued. It was always the same. It was the bloody trial judge's fault. It was a lousy charge—unfair, biased, hopeless, or a combination of the aforementioned.

Always, counsel's skill had secured the victory.

Always, the defeat was the fault of the trial judge.

But then, not infrequently, I too had silently cursed the trial judge whose lacklustre charge was weighted heavily in favour of the defence.

The judge's summing-up of the facts and the law at the close of counsels' speeches is a vitally important part of trial by jury. It has been said that jurors have a right to expect from the judge something more than a mere repetition of the evidence. They have a right to expect his or her trained legal mind will employ itself in stripping the testimony of non-essentials to present clearly the evidence that requires factual decision, the case put forward by the prosecution, and the answer of the defence, or such answer as the evidence permits.

Sir James F. Stephen was an English jurist and journalist who was born in 1829. Undoubtedly his most famous work was his *History of the Criminal Law of England* which he completed in 1883. However, it was 20 years earlier that he had written *A General View of the Criminal Law* wherein he reflected upon the necessary ingredients for a proper charge. He wrote, in part:

"I think that a judge who merely states to the jury certain propositions of law and then reads over his notes does not discharge his duty. I also think that a judge who forms a decided opinion before he has heard the whole case, or who allows himself to be, in any degree, actuated by an advocate's feelings, in regulating the proceedings, altogether fails to discharge his duty; but, I further think that he ought not to conceal his opinion from the jury, nor do I see how it is possible for him to do so, if he arranges the evidence in the order in which it strikes his mind. The mere effort to see what is essential to a story, in what order the important events happened, and in what relation they stand to each other, must of necessity point to some conclusion. The act of stating for the jury the question which they have to answer and of stating the evidence bearing on these questions and shewing in what respects it is important, generally goes a considerable way towards suggesting an answer to them; and, if a judge does not do as much at least as this, he does almost nothing."

Thursday, May 1, 1986

At precisely 9:32 a.m., Madam Justice Krindle was well into the general part of her charge.

"You are neither partisans nor advocates," she told the jurors. "You are judges and your contribution to the administration of justice is a just and proper verdict. You must approach your duties objectively with neither pity nor sympathy for the accused, nor prejudice or passion against him.

"In determining the guilt or innocence of the accused, you are to be governed solely by the evidence introduced in this trial and by the law and absolutely nothing else."

She spoke to them about the presumption of innocence, of reasonable doubt and burden of proof, of circumstantial evidence and inferences that could be drawn from proven facts. Her words were simple words, spoken with crystal clarity. Twelve alert judges of the facts, their eyes glued on the face of the diminutive jurist, heard what she said. And they understood.

Once the general principles of the law had been addressed, Krindle began her meticulous analysis of the case for the Crown and defence.

"Before I charge you on the law relative to murder, I would like to deal with that evidence which may go to the issue of whether or not it was the accused who was, for want of a better word at this point, Ruby Adriaenssens' assailant. I will use, for convenience, some of the same headings which Ms. Keyser used yesterday in her argument to you.

"There was discussion about evidence of opportunity. I mentioned to you earlier when we were discussing the weight to be attached to the testimony of witnesses, there are a variety of factors to be borne in mind, one of which was as follows: Did the witnesses have any particular reason to assist them in recalling a precise event that he or she has attempted to describe? Or could the witness, because of the relative unimportance of the event at the time it occurred, be easily and understandably in error as to detail?

"You have heard from Ferlon Goosehead and Corrine Demas as to the time they believe they went to the Maryland on the evening of September the 13th. Was there any particular reason shown to you why time was important to them on that Friday night? Or was the actual time reasonably unimportant then, at the time that it occurred, and it only became important later? Let me show you what I mean.

"Ferlon states that he estimates that it was between 8:30 and 8:45 when the accused left the Maryland Hotel. Corrine Demas has them arriving at the Maryland Hotel at about 8:15 in the evening. Ms. Keyser pointed both of those times out to you yesterday. But there are other witnesses as to the time other than Ferlon and Corrine Demas. Janet Green says the accused left the Maryland around eight o'clock in that evening. Ron Schweid has the accused at the table in the Maryland when he arrived, which was about eight o'clock in the evening. Eva Courchene said the accused and Ferlon joined her table at about 10 minutes to eight in the evening. Sharon James, the accused's sister, said that, when she spoke to the accused on the Saturday morning, he told her he left the Maryland a little after eight o'clock. He also told her he left with Corrine Demas.

"It is for you to decide what, if anything, to do with evidence of time. It is for you to decide if anyone is lying. In my opinion, I do not think anyone is deliberately trying to mislead. Time was not very important to those people. Nobody was looking at their watch and recording times. They did not have any reason to be paying particular attention to time. It did not become significant, not until at least 24 hours later when the police started speaking to them. And then everybody tried, in my opinion, to come up with their best estimate. They tried to reconstruct. And they could very well be wrong. Not dishonest, but wrong.

"Shirley Adriaenssens was timing her bread. She was paying attention to a clock. Her evidence is that she went downstairs with Ruby at eight o'clock because her bread was going to be ready and it was in the oven. There is a reason for her to remember eight o'clock. Thereafter, she, and later Tania, are estimating. By their own testimony they are estimating, and they are estimating in an area, again, which only later becomes significant....

"Another area that Ms. Keyser raised and that has to be discussed is what she called the evidence of John James's lies—I believe that was the heading that she called it; that was the heading I wrote it down as—and what you do with that testimony, what inferences you can draw from it. There were certain lies which she admitted, she as counsel for Mr. James, admitted in her address to you, were deliberate falsehoods. I will accept, in my charge to you, the defence position and will treat those comments as being deliberate falsehoods.

"The first area in which the accused admittedly lied, according to his counsel, was in phone conversation with Sharon James, his sister, the next morning. Sharon James testified that, on the Saturday morning, she asked her brother what he had done the previous evening. He said he had met Corrine Demas at the Maryland and had left with her shortly after eight o'clock in the evening to go to Stanley's on Burrows. Ms. Keyser has acknowledged that the accused lied to his sister when he said he left the Maryland with Corrine Demas. She explains the lie as being a little brother showing off to his sister about his gallantries and success with the young lady. That may well be so. It is for you to decide. But there is another falsehood in what the accused told his sister. He did not, according to the evidence you have heard, meet Corrine Demas in the Maryland. Rather, he met her at the Inglis Block, at the Gouvreaus' suite, in the same block from which, a short time later, Ruby Adriaenssens went missing. The Crown says the accused omitted reference to the Inglis Block, to the Gouvreaus' suite, for the same reason that the accused lied about what he did on leaving the Maryland. Because that block, and his conduct on leaving the Maryland, were areas about which he felt a consciousness of guilt on that Saturday morning and he felt fear arising out of his own misconduct. Again, that is for you to consider.

"The next area in which John James admittedly lied is in his initial dealings with Mr. Gove and Sergeant Preisentanz. You will recall that, when they got to the house, the first question Mr. Gove put to John James—this is Saturday about seven—was:

"Who were you with last night?'

"John James's immediate response—and he is still at Harry James's house at this time; he has not been asked to leave—was:

"'My sister Sharon.'

"According to Sharon, he had not been with her that previous evening. It is for you to determine what you draw from the fact that, to a perfectly innocuous question like that, while he is still with his Uncle Harry, while he has not been taken down to the Public Safety Building, John James would lie about who he was with the previous evening.

"At the Public Safety Building, there was a verbal exchange between Mr. Gove and Sergeant Preisentanz on the one hand, and John James on the other. The officers recorded the conversation in their notebooks. You will not have a written statement with you as to exactly what was said. You will have the later written statement that was taken, but the verbal exchange that preceded it, you will have to rely on your recollection of the testimony of the witnesses. I think it is advisable, because this is a significant area, that I just read to you the questions and answers upon John James being taken into the Public Safety Building simply to refresh your memory as to what Sergeant Preisentanz said the dialogue was.

Question: 'Could you tell us what you did last night?'
Answer: 'Well, I worked until 3:30.'
Q: 'Then what?'
A: 'I went to my cousin's on Wellington.'
Q: 'What time?'
A: 'Around four o'clock.'
Q: 'What is his name?'
A: 'Michael James.'
Q: 'Then what?'
A: 'Around 4:30 we went to the Maryland.'
Q: 'Who with?'
A: 'Ferlon Goosehead.'
Constable Gove then said: 'Did you not say Sinclair?'
A: 'Yes, both Goosehead or Sinclair he is called. We were asked for ID and left.'
Q: 'Then what?'
A: 'Around five o'clock we left and went to the Northern. We left here around six and went to the Sutherland.'

Q: 'Then what?'

A: 'Around 6:30 we went to the West. Then went walking on Main with Ferlon. We then went to the Patricia.'

Q: 'What time was that?'

A: 'Around 7:30. We then left and went to the McLaren. Ferlon stayed and I went to the development on Burrows. I went to my cousin's, Stanley James's.'

Q: 'What time did you get there?'

A: 'Around 8:30.'

Q: 'Then what?'

A: 'We walked to the 7-Eleven on McPhillips and then to McDonald's. We went back to Mountain and I took a bus home.'

Q: 'Then what?'

A: 'I met Eileen McKinney and we went to the Sutherland.'

Q: 'What time was this?'

A: 'Around 9:15. We had one beer and I went home to bed. I was pretty drunk.'

"That," the judge noted, "is the dialogue between the accused and the police officers immediately upon the accused's arrival at the Public Safety Building.

"Ms. Keyser argues that the accused would have felt threatened in the presence of the police officers, particularly in light of his not knowing why he was there. She suggests to you that perhaps he thought it was because he had tried to kiss Corrine the night before he was in the police station. Ms. Keyser postulates that the accused deliberately denied having been in the company of Corrine or in any one of those places because of that fear.

"When you go over that statement, you will note that there is something missing and counsel has agreed it is missing. What is missing in that statement is all reference to having been at the Gouvreaus' suite which is in the Inglis Block, which is also the block in which Ruby Adriaenssens lived. What is missing from that statement is all reference to being at the Maryland Hotel about eight o'clock that evening with Corrine Demas, with Ferlon Goosehead, with anybody. It is just not there. What is missing in that statement is what the accused did on leaving the

Maryland Hotel. There is no reference to that either because there is no reference to him having been at the Maryland Hotel. According to that statement...he and Ferlon went to the McLaren at 7:30. Ferlon stayed and he, the accused, went to Stanley James's.

"Those are the elements that are missing. They are, counsel concedes, deliberately misleading. It is for you to determine in your own mind why, when the accused talked to the police at the Public Safety Building on the Saturday, he left out reference to where he was between a quarter to eight and, say, 8:30 on the night before. He left out reference to the Inglis Block; he left out reference to the Maryland Hotel.

"You have Ms. Keyser's explanation that she urges you to accept.

"You also have the Crown's position. James was lying in an attempt to mislead the police as to his whereabouts because of consciousness of guilt.

"You will have to come to grips with this. You will have to think about it. You will have to decide what inference is to be drawn from that deliberate falsehood in the initial conversation with Preisentanz and Gove. Bring your common sense to bear in your analysis of the reasons why the accused might have lied as he did.

"Finally, there is the admitted lie about Eli Tacan—after the police had finally told the accused what it was they were investigating, after they told him—and these are the words that they used—'We told him we were investigating the death of a little girl in that block.'

"That is what the accused was told by police.

"Ms. Keyser has painted for you a picture of a young person in a state of panic who does something irrational, something stupid; who invents a story about someone else who supposedly confessed to the accused in order to divert from himself what he believes is police suspicion of him. It is for you to ask yourself whether that type of behaviour is consistent with your human experience and would it explain the lie.

"The Crown's position as I understand it is, however, that

even if the explanation is true, even if the accused made up the whole Eli Tacan story because he was frightened and panicking and he was in a police situation, there is something in what he told the police that could only have been told to the police by someone who had been present when the little girl was killed. He told the police that Eli Tacan told him that he, Eli Tacan, had taken the little girl from the block, had taken her down to a garage two blocks away down the lane and the little girl was crying for her grandmother.

"How did he know those facts if he had not been there? How did he even know that the little girl had a grandmother? How did he know to say to the police, in the midst of this fabrication about Eli Tacan, that the little girl was crying for her grandmother? The Crown says to you, as I understand counsel's position, that, by saying those words, the accused is acknowledging that he was at the scene. He is acknowledging that he knows that this little girl died in a back lane, in a garage two blocks away from the apartment block where she lived, crying for her grandmother.

"I consider that comment to be significant. It is for you to decide what to do with it. It may be simply that the accused fabricated it like he fabricated the whole business about Eli Tacan. But isn't that a bit close? Isn't that a bit coincidental? I leave it to you.

"Later on, in the written statement which you will have with you when you retire to consider your verdict, the accused repeats it.

"'Then he, Eli, came back and he started to tell me about it. He said he saw a little girl walking up toward the third floor.'

"You know from the grandmother that she probably was walking up toward the third floor. But how did the accused know it? Not from Eli Tacan. His lawyer has conceded that that is a fairy-tale. How did the accused know that?

"'He grabbed her and took off with her. He grabbed her and went to a garage two blocks away. He said the little girl was crying for her grandmother.'

"People in a trapped position, perfectly innocent people in

a trapped position, can lie. And a young man in a police station feeling threatened with the possibility of a murder charge could very well make up a lie to the police. He could say, 'I don't know, police, why are you investigating me? Eli Tacan told me he killed the little girl.' That, certainly. But what, ladies and gentlemen of the jury, do you do with those details? How does he know those details? That is essentially the Crown's position on what you are to draw, the inference you are to draw, from the false statements of the accused.

"There is, finally, the admission of the accused. This was made after four hours in custody, or in the police station, in any event. It was made to two officers. And Ms. Keyser says you should be careful as to the weight that you attach to it. You have heard her argue on that point. She argued—well, she argued forcibly. Consider that....

"There is, then, testimony concerning the hair and fibre samples. I do not intend to go over this in detail with you. You heard the hair and fibre man a couple of days ago. Each of the lawyers went through the hair and fibre analysis in some considerable detail with you yesterday. I would point out simply a few things that I recall from the testimony that I think are significant.

"Number one: When Mr. Cadieux was on the stand, you will recall that I asked him a question about washing clothes. His answer went beyond just washing clothes. He said:

"'Fibres will come off in the course of washing. Fibres will fall off if the clothes are being worn.'

"The accused was wearing the leather jacket and the black cap. They were not washed. At least I do not expect they were washed. Do you consider it significant that no fibres from the child's clothes were on a leather jacket or cap? He also mentioned, I believe, in the course of his testimony, the kind of material that it is would have a lot to do with whether fibres even stick to it to begin with. The leather jacket is a leather jacket. Exercise your common sense on that.

"Insofar as the remaining matters are concerned, the only other thing I feel I should repeat for you is Mr. Cadieux's own comments about the worth of hair analysis. He said, and I quote:

"'It is my experience, and that of other experts, that coincidental matches in human hair comparisons are relatively rare events. The chance that the questioned hair did indeed originate from the same source as the known sample is by far the more likely of the two possibilities.'

"There were, on or about the person of little Ruby Adriaenssens, and on the cinder block, hairs that corresponded in all particulars with those of the accused. There were, on the clothing of the accused, on his sock and on the black T-shirt, two hairs that corresponded with those of Ruby Adriaenssens. Are you prepared to say that is mere coincidence?

"Insofar as fibres are concerned, I don't intend to go through all of this again with you, because I am sure it is fresh in your mind. What Mr. Cadieux said was that it was the combination of fibres that he found to be significant. Black polyester and cotton are not unusual. But when fibres match up with the sweatpants and with the T-shirt and with the cuffs on the jacket and with the hat, are you prepared to simply say that might be coincidence?

"At the end of the whole of your analysis of the evidence, at the end of your looking at hair and fibres, at the end of your asking yourself what inferences you are prepared to draw, if any, from the false statements, at the end of your analysis of the inculpatory statement in which John James admits to having grabbed the girl and dragged her down the back lane, at the end of all that, you must ask yourself if the Crown has convinced you, beyond a reasonable doubt, that it is John James, and none other, who was the assailant of little Ruby Adriaenssens.

"If you are satisfied beyond a reasonable doubt that it was John James, you will go ahead with your consideration of what offences the evidence discloses, which is what I will be getting to next.

"If you have a doubt, and it is a reasonable one, then you must exercise it in his favour and acquit.

"It is the totality of that evidence that you must look at. You look at it piece by piece, but you also look at it finally in its totality and ask yourself whether it convinces you, beyond a reasonable doubt, that it was John James who was Ruby Adriaenssens' assailant. And, as I said, if you have a doubt, and if it is a reasonable one, then you must acquit totally. You would go no further."

The recess, however brief, brought relief in one form or another to all. Court was now back in session.

"Members of the jury," Krindle smiled and said, "I would now like to direct you on the law as it relates to the charge of murder. May I first deal with the area of culpable homicide which, in 20th-century English, just means a blameworthy death or blameworthy killing.

"A person commits homicide when, directly or indirectly, by any means, he causes the death of a human being....

"A person commits culpable homicide when he causes the death of a human being by means of an unlawful act. An assault is an unlawful act. I direct you that, whoever it was that caused the death of Ruby Adriaenssens, there is no question but that that person committed culpable homicide.

"There are certain circumstances where you can cause the death of a human being and it is not blameworthy. Self-defence is one of them; accident is another. There is no suggestion, on the facts of this case, that either of those defences might arise. How can it be self-defence when you are dealing with a three-year-old? It is culpable homicide. It is the death of a human being caused by means of an unlawful act.

"Culpable homicide is murder in two distinct situations. It is murder where a person causes the death of a human being while committing or attempting to commit a sexual assault, whether or not that person means to cause death to any human being, and whether or not he knows that death is likely to be caused to any human being if he means to cause bodily harm for the purpose of (a) facilitating the commission of a sexual assault, or (b) facilitating his flight after committing or attempting to commit sexual assault.

"Let me go through that with you again, a bit more slowly

this time. Culpable homicide is murder where a person causes the death of a human being while committing or attempting to commit a sexual assault. All right? It is murder where a person causes the death of another human being while committing or attempting to commit sexual assault. That is the first half of it."

I had, over the years, listened to judges, some two and three decades senior to Krindle, charge a jury on the law of homicide. The jurors, at times, were left as perplexed as if the judge had attempted to explain gravitation, electromagnetism and sub-atomic phenomena in one set of rules.

These jurors, I observed, were not confused.

"Now," Krindle asked, "what evidence is before you with respect to sexual assault? And what evidence is before you with respect to whether death was caused while committing or attempting to commit sexual assault? You will recall the testimony of Dr. Markesteyn and Dr. McRae who examined the child at the post-mortem. Both doctors observed bruising and slight tears around the child's rectum. In their opinion, based on their experience—and you heard their experience and you heard their qualifications—that bruising of the child's rectum was consistent with an attempt at anal penetration of the child....

"Now, sexual assault is a word that I have used. An assault is simply an application of force by one person to the person of another without the consent of that other. And I can tell you, in the case of Ruby, that, all other things aside, she is too young in law to ever be able to consent. That is what an assault is. Sexual assault is an assault in a sexual context, with a sexual connotation, either done for the purpose of sexually gratifying the assailant or done with a sexual object in mind. It is simply an assault with an element of sexuality attached to it.

"If you find that there was attempted anal penetration, in a sexual context, you are entitled to find that there was an attempted sexual assault or a sexual assault. The doctors aren't certain whether there was total penetration or not, but the assault was there. The rectum had been assaulted, albeit perhaps not fully, not totally, not with ejaculation, but enough to bruise

139

it; enough to make tiny tears on it that Dr. Markesteyn observed, and one tear at the nine o'clock position observed by Dr. McRae.

"The evidence given by the doctors, if you accept it, and if you accept the inference to be drawn from it, is such that it is capable of amounting to evidence of sexual assault.

"All right. Now let me go back to my definition of murder again.

"Culpable homicide is murder where a person causes the death of a human being while committing or attempting to commit sexual assault. When was the death of Ruby Adriaenssens caused? Was it caused while the person was committing or attempting to commit sexual assault? The Crown, having laid this charge, must prove each and every one of the elements of it beyond a reasonable doubt, including the fact that death was caused during the commission of or an attempt to commit a sexual assault.

"Dr. Markesteyn was able to tell you certain things. He explained the injuries to the head. It was the injuries to the head which caused the death, not the anal injuries. The anal injuries were basically superficial. And, he said that, in his opinion, death was almost instantaneous with the injuries to the head. He also said that the injuries to the rectum occurred just before, at the time of, or immediately after death.

"I will repeat that for you.

"The injuries to the head, according to Dr. Markesteyn, caused death almost immediately. The injuries to the rectum occurred just before, at the time of, or just after death.

"Dr. Markesteyn times the injuries to the rectum by the fact that there was no healing. He said in his testimony that, if a person had lived after the injuries, the body would have started the healing process. He also said that it would be just after death because there was bruising. If there had been the passage of time, there would not have been blood around the rectum to bruise. Bruising is the passing of blood out of the blood vessels and into the system.

"The evidence is before you. Does that evidence satisfy you beyond a reasonable doubt that death was caused while committing or attempting to commit a sexual assault?

"Now, if you are satisfied of that, it does not matter whether the person who assaulted young Ruby meant to cause death to her, whether he knew that death was likely to be caused to her. And you must find this. He means to cause bodily harm for the purpose of either facilitating the commission of the offence or, alternatively, facilitating his flight, his escape, after committing or attempting to commit the offence, and death ensues from the bodily harm. The bodily harm from which death ensued were the injuries, the blows to the head. I am not going to describe them for you. Dr. Markesteyn described them graphically and the pictures show them clearly.

"Are you satisfied that the accused meant to cause bodily harm for the purpose of facilitating the commission of the offence of sexual assault or facilitating his escape after committing or attempting to commit the offence of sexual assault and death ensued from the bodily harm? Has the Crown satisfied you of that beyond a reasonable doubt?

"Now we are here talking about what the accused meant to do. Did he mean to cause bodily harm? In that regard, you may wish to look at the photographs and see what he actually did. You may wish to review Dr. Markesteyn's testimony as to the type of force that would have been necessary to cause that kind of bodily harm to the child.

"You may also rely on a very common-sense inference which is that people normally intend the logical consequences, the natural consequences, of their acts. If somebody took the head of a youngster and smashed it up against a brick, it is a reasonable inference that he would mean to cause bodily harm to the youngster. However, I am speaking of an inference. It is not absolute that he would mean to cause it. It is simply a common-sense inference that you can draw."

Some counsel scribble furiously during the course of a judge's charge; some listen attentively; others daydream. Some look at the jurors occasionally as I had done. Always, I noticed, the eyes of each juror were riveted on the face of the young jurist.

"One of the things I think you must look at," Krindle continued, "when you are dealing with this inference that a person intends the natural consequences of his acts, is the question of alcohol and the effect that the consumption of alcohol may have had on the ability of the accused to mean, to intend. Evidence has been given that the accused had consumed alcohol prior to the incident in question.

"According to Eva Courchene, who sat next to him at the Maryland, he was perfectly intelligible. He walked in a totally normal way. He did not appear to her to be drunk in any way. According to Ferlon Goosehead, he and the accused were not drunk. Ferlon had been with the accused since after work. Ferlon said they had a beer at the Maryland, one beer and a rye and Coke at the Northern. They split a jug at the Leland and they had a beer later. That is the consumption, between about 4 p.m. and 8 p.m., according to Ferlon Goosehead.

"Neither Eva nor Ferlon knew the accused well. That is something that you should consider. I think he was a total stranger to Eva and I believe that Ferlon said that he had not met him before that particular day. So that their opinion as to his sobriety is something that you should weigh with caution.

"However, at 9:15 that evening according to the accused, at 9:30 according to Eileen McKinney, they met in front of 89 Lorne Avenue and walked to the Northern for a drink. According to all of the evidence, Eileen McKinney was totally sober at the time. She lives with Harry James. The accused lives with Harry James. It was defence counsel herself who, on cross-examination, had Eileen McKinney agree that about 9:30 that evening, an approximate hour, I would think, after the incident in question, that the accused seemed to her to be perfectly normal.

"According to the accused, in terms of what he said to Corrine Demas, he told Corrine he was drunk. He also told police officers that he was drunk. And he makes mention in one of his statements of having blacked out. He also makes mention in one of his statements, and I leave this to you for what it is worth, that he smoked a couple of joints in the bathroom of the Maryland Hotel with Eli Tacan, who was not there. I point out to you that that evidence of consumption of alcohol by the accused and perhaps smoking a couple of joints exists. You will have to think about it.

"As I said, the accused in his statement to the police says that he was drunk and that he was blacking out. Corrine Demas says he told her he was drunk.

"It is for you to weigh the evidence of drunkenness. Think about what Ferlon Goosehead said. Think about what Eva Courchene had said. Eva was sitting next to him in the Maryland. I would think particularly about what Eileen McKinney says about his state of sobriety at 9:30 at night. And then think about what the accused himself has said.

"Very often, as your own experience will tell you, people sometimes try to excuse their own actions by saying, 'I was drunk. I don't remember.' However, that may not be the case. There is evidence of drink. And I have recited what Ferlon says they drank.

"The mere fact that a person was drunk is not, in itself, a defence to a criminal prosecution. In this case, to the extent that you may find on the evidence that the accused had been drinking, and I think the evidence is clear that he had been drinking, you may consider the fact of his drinking along with all of the other facts as you find them on the evidence in determining whether the accused had the intent necessary.

"Did the accused mean to cause bodily harm for the purpose of sexually assaulting the youngster? Or, did he mean to cause bodily harm for the purpose of facilitating his flight?

"When you are making a finding, as you must in this case, as to the accused's intent, remember, he has to mean to cause bodily harm.

"If, on the evidence before you, you find that the accused was so drunk that he was incapable of forming the intent to cause bodily harm, then you may not convict him of murder. You would, in that event, convict of manslaughter.

"If you find that the accused was capable of forming the intent, you have to find, as well, and be satisfied beyond a reasonable doubt, that he meant to cause bodily harm, because a person can have the capacity without having the intent.

"If the accused had the capacity to form the intent, and had the intent to cause bodily harm, and death resulted from that bodily harm, it is no defence that the accused acted in the way he did because of drink or that he would not have acted in that way had he been sober.

"We are not here concerned with whether drink caused him to do things that he would not do if he were sober. The concern here is this: Are you satisfied that he meant to cause bodily harm? Or, was he so drunk that he was incapable of meaning to cause bodily harm?

"A man may be drunk to a high degree and yet be able to form the intent to act as he does. The fact that his mind was so affected by drink that he more readily gave way to some violent passion or to temptation provides no defence if he had the requisite intent for murder.

"As I have already mentioned, you must take into account all the surrounding circumstances in deciding whether the accused had the requisite intent, whether he meant to cause bodily harm for the purpose of facilitating the commission of the sexual assault, or whether he meant to cause bodily harm for the purpose of facilitating his flight after committing or attempting to commit the offence of sexual assault and death ensues from the bodily harm."

The trial judge was nearing the end of her instructions.

"There is another section with respect to murder...," she informed the jurors.

"If you have a doubt as to whether the murder occurred while the accused was committing or attempting to commit sexual assault, only then would you go to this section. This section, if you find it to have been proved, is not murder in the first degree; it is second degree murder. Murder while committing or attempting to commit sexual assault is first degree murder.

"Now, dealing with second degree murder, the Crown must prove beyond a reasonable doubt, firstly, that the accused caused the death of Ruby Adriaenssens. That feature is the same in first and second degree murder. The Crown must then prove beyond a reasonable doubt that the accused meant to cause Ruby Adriaenssens bodily harm, that he knew the bodily harm was likely to cause her death, and was reckless as to whether death ensued or not....

"If you have a doubt as to whether murder occurred during the course of a sexual assault, but you are satisfied that murder occurred, you will find the accused not guilty of first degree murder but guilty of second degree murder.

"If you have a doubt as to whether the accused was able to form the intention to commit second degree murder, he was so drunk that he could not mean to cause bodily harm, that he could not know that death was a likely result, if you have a doubt about that, then you will find the accused not guilty of murder but guilty of manslaughter."

At the end of the charge, the trial judge may receive from the jury room a request in the form of a question, for clarification on a point of law. More often than not in murder trials, it was my experience that jurors wanted the judge to extricate them from the web of mass confusion that he or she had woven around the allowable verdicts. Jurors always seemed to get tangled up in the strands between manslaughter and murder one and murder two.

I knew these jurors were not confused. There would not be any questions about their options. I looked up at Krindle and thought, with much satisfaction, that she was as good as the best of the old-timers.

"I have prepared a verdict sheet and the clerk has copies with her," Krindle said. "I am going to ask her to give those copies to you to take with you into the jury room. They simply outline the four potential verdicts that are open to you in this case. Number one, a verdict of not guilty. Number two, a verdict of guilty as charged. In other words, guilty of first degree murder. Guilty of murder during the course of commission of a sexual assault. Number three, not guilty of first degree murder but guilty of second degree murder. And, number four, not guilty of murder but guilty of manslaughter.

"There is no magic in the order in which I have set out those potential verdicts. I am not attempting to signal anything by it. They are set out in the order in which I dealt with things in my charge.

"When you return your verdict, that verdict sheet may help you in conveying your verdict to the court in wording that is sufficiently precise that we will not have any difficulty in understanding your verdict....

"As I stated to you at the outset, you must be unanimous in your verdict. It is the right of a jury to disagree, but I know you will do your best to come to an agreement. This trial has involved time, expense, disruption of your lives and disruption of the lives of the witnesses. I am certain that no other 12 people could deal with this matter better than you can. If there is anything about which you are not clear, either in terms of the applicable law or the evidence, I will be available to answer your questions. If you have any questions, would your foreman put them in writing and give them to the constable.

"You have taken an oath to well and truly try this charge and to render a true verdict according to the evidence. If you honour that oath, you will have done all that is expected of you.

"I would like to thank you very much for the attention you have paid during this matter.

"Would you swear in the constables, please."

Two sheriff's officers, who would attend to the needs and wants of the jurors during their deliberations, were sworn in.

Tough lawyers, even the most robust, wilt before a murder trial is over. Now, as this solemn inquiry into the truth was nearing its finale, limp and drooping counsel heard those soothing, long-awaited words of deliverance: "Members of the jury, you may now retire and consider your verdict."

Protestations

As the door to the jury room was closing, Keyser was getting to her feet.

"My lady," she said, "perhaps the jury members should be told not to start their deliberations until we have had an opportunity to address you with respect to the charge."

Counsel's intrusion into judicial territory was met with mild tolerance.

"I do not mind if they start their deliberations," the judge said impassively. "I do not think we will be here that dreadfully long. I suspect they will be going for lunch soon."

She invited counsels' comments on her charge.

With each passing day, I found myself frequently reliving my colourful yesterdays. At that particular moment, I was relishing the reminiscence of a judicial rebuke I had received long ago. The late Mr. Justice John M. Hunt, a modest and most excellent man, had completed his charge and had asked counsel for their observations.

"A most exemplary charge, my lord," I sang out, "one deserving of no further comment."

His lordship lowered his eyes and said nothing at the time. Later, he cautioned me that there never was, nor would there ever be, an exemplary charge. And so, while he was most appreciative of the felicitous remark, he suggested that the more prudent course would have been to say nothing.

"Might I hear from Crown counsel?" Krindle inquired.

As I got to my feet, I resolved that this time it will be different.

"My lady, for me, that was a very thorough charge. It was a very thoughtful charge. In a word, it was an exemplary charge."

The judge lowered her eyes and said nothing.

To suggest Keyser was disenchanted would be a gross understatement.

"My lady, I have some serious concerns about the charge to the jury," the grim-faced counsel announced passionately, "and there are a number of factors I wish to address because of that.

"Firstly, at the outset, you indicated to the jury that, often, pride would make members of a jury reticent about bending to the will of other jurors. And I am not certain that the jurors were impressed that they have an absolute right to hold onto their opinions if they feel strongly about them. In fact, they have a duty to do so if they believe that their position is, in fact, correct, notwithstanding the arguments of the other jurors."

Krindle interjected: "I think the question dealt with taking a rigid position at the outset."

"Yes," Keyser agreed, "but I do not believe at any point during the charge it was stressed that—"

"No, it wasn't."

"—they have an absolute right to hold onto an opinion, regardless of the opinions of 11 other jurors, if they feel strongly about their position. That was one of my concerns."

Krindle smiled and said, "Okay."

At that particular moment, I had been thinking about Isaac Walton—"the gentlest teacher and powerfullest preacher"—on the gentle art of angling. What a profound joy it was to cast my eye from the bench to the other end of the counsel table and watch the master angler addressing the trout.

Keyser was not at all happy with the manner in which the court had dealt with testimony concerning the time that James was alleged to have arrived at, and departed from, the Maryland Hotel.

"Secondly," she complained, "when you dealt with the aspect of time for their consideration, you indicated that they should consider whether time was important to the people who were giving the times. And I submit that there is no evidence that the people who gave the times had any reason not to remember the times, whether or not the times were unimportant to them.

"And, if you are going to be dealing with specific times given by individuals, I think it should have been stressed that the other people at the Maryland, Eva Courchene, Ronald Schweid and Janet Green, had even less reason to remember the time than the individuals that Mr. James went to the Maryland with. I have some concerns about dealing with the aspect of time because, as you could see from my address to the jury, that was one of the pivotal points of the defence."

Krindle listened, but said nothing. Counsel moved to another area of critical concern to the defence.

"When my lady dealt with the aspect of the details given to the police by Mr. James, albeit attributed to Eli Tacan, Mr. James's explanation for knowing those details was also given to the police. Eileen had told him about the little girl. There is no explanation, there is no evidence as to the extent of the knowledge that had been imparted, or when it had been imparted to him by Eileen. She was called by the Crown and she was not examined on that. And that is a very, very important factor, I suggest.

"My feeling was that the position of the Crown was stressed unduly in your dealings with those details to the detriment of the defence."

The judge listened, but still said nothing. Counsel then addressed the court's treatment of the hair and fibre samples, saying, among other things:

"And, as well, when you put to them Mr. Cadieux's comments about the relatively rare incidence of accidental matches, I believe it also should have been stressed that that is his particular opinion, but that there are other experts who disagree with the value of hair evidence. And I believe that his testimony was in fact given too much weight in terms of his particular position, without stressing that other experts do not necessarily agree with his position.

"As well, in dealing with the particular hair and fibre matches, what was stressed was the elements of the hair and fibre testimony that potentially matched Mr. James's, but not all of the problems with respect to the hair and fibre evidence. And that was not stressed enough to the jury, I suggest."

At last, Krindle spoke.

"I do not think, Ms. Keyser, that, on that score, I even particularly stressed what they found where. I think that my treatment of the hair and fibre, if anything, was cursory. But so much attention had been given to it yesterday, and the witness was so recent, that I just did not bother to repeat either the Crown or defence version of where the hairs were."

A distressed Kee leaned toward me.

"As long as they're on their feet, the meter keeps running," he snorted.

Keyser persisted.

"My feeling, my lady, was that it was not an exhaustive attempt to go through the thing for obvious reasons, because we have heard it recently. But what was stressed was evidence that aided the prosecution and not the evidence that came out, I suggest, quite strongly in favour of the defence."

The judge nodded, but said nothing further.

Counsel then suggested that the court had failed to bring home strongly enough to the jury certain features that distinguished first degree murder from second.

Finally, it was counsel's contention that it had not been stressed enough to the jurors that they had to be satisfied beyond a reasonable doubt that the person accused was the person responsible.

It was the only time throughout the trial that Krindle lost patience with counsel.

"I thought that, before we broke for coffee," the judge said tersely, "and I really tried to stress this, that they had to be satisfied beyond a reasonable doubt that the accused was the right guy; that, if they had any doubt, then they stopped, and acquitted."

"You did that, my lady," Keyser conceded plaintively. "I am just not certain it was stressed enough from my point."

The court heard Crown counsel's response without comment.

"Ms. Keyser," Krindle then said, "the areas that you mentioned were areas that I had considered at the time I prepared the charge. I tried to balance them as well as I could. Under the circumstances, I am not prepared to recall the jury on any of those issues.

"The charge, in terms of the law, I found it a difficult one to prepare for them. Those sections do not lend themselves to easy explanation, unfortunately, and neither does the law as to intent. But, I do not think, under the circumstances, that I am prepared to recall the jury and recharge them. We are talking stress and details, not anything of substance. And I am going to leave the charge as it stands."

The sternness then dissipated and was replaced by the customary cheerfulness. Court was adjourned pending the verdict of the jury.

CHAPTER 13

The Verdict

There was a question from the jury room.

The clerk alerted the judge, rounded up the lawyers, and herded all of them back into the courtroom by 1:50 p.m.

Krindle read the question aloud:

"My lady, what happened to the hair from Ruby's mouth and hands?"

Discussion followed. The Crown attorneys had read nothing in the police or autopsy reports concerning what had happened to that hair. The judge and counsel checked their notes and searched their memories. The proposed answer, all conceded, would be unsatisfactory at best.

The jury was recalled.

"I have read your question to counsel, ladies and gentlemen," Krindle told them. "Before you came in, I had a chance to go through my notes in this area and to discuss it with counsel.

"The evidence is unclear as to whether those hairs from the hands and mouth formed part of the body tapings or not. If the hairs from the mouth and hands were separate from the body tapings, the evidence is silent as to what may have happened to them.

"I know that that does not answer your question. All I can do is refer to the evidence as it was given in court. You have to base your verdict on the evidence as you heard it. And that, as unclear as it may be, is the evidence."

The jurors nodded collectively. Court adjourned at 2:15 p.m.

The prosecutors and a small police contingent manoeuvred their way out of the courtroom, through the crowded corridors, down two flights of stairs and deep into the entrails of the old Law Courts Building. It is always cool down there. Nestled among the foundation stones, there is a marvellous secret sanctuary—an oak-panelled lounge where Crown counsel and police find refuge.

Counsel wearily tossed their robes and vests and tabs onto a long mahogany table. One vest missed its mark and hit the floor. Nobody bothered to pick it up. Kee kicked off his polished loafers, stretched out languidly on one of the oversized blue leather chesterfields and shut his eyes.

For those who practise in the criminal courts, the long vigil before verdict is dead time, non-productive and frustrating. Self-doubt frequently overtakes them. The pressure builds.

Sergeant Angus Anderson had learned to cope effectively with stress. He prided himself on his capacity to assist others in alleviating their post-trial tensions. Magically, he produced relief in the form of a squat, cut-glass bottle containing a rich amber fluid. The ever-faithful Calvin Osborne was there beside his sergeant, anxious, as always, to serve. This time, it was ice cubes.

Kee gratefully accepted a glass from Osborne, sat up and savoured two long swallows. Then, staring intently into his glass, he allowed as how Ruthie Krindle had just delivered one hell of a fine charge to the jury.

Glasses were clinked together. There was a chorus of approbation. Then Kee put his glass on the floor and appeared to fall asleep.

Darryl Preisentanz's right fist exploded into the palm of his left hand. "What the hell happened to the hair that was found in the little kid's mouth and hands?" he demanded loudly to no one in particular. "The bloody press will have a field day with that one, you can bet your ass."

"I think we're in for a long wait," somebody grumbled.

"Naw," said another, "you'll be home in time to watch *The Young and the Restless*, Darryl."

The big sergeant's instant response, an invitation to perform a rather impossible physical act, was drowned out in a chorus of merry guffaws. More idle speculation and inconsequential jabber followed. Then, as the ever-considerate Anderson started refilling a glass, a banging fist struck the solid oak door.

"You've got a verdict," shouted Alfie Wilkes, the gravel-throated, barrel-chested sheriff's officer.

"Let's move it," he ordered as he marched through the door.

Alfie looked tough and liked to talk tough. He was a Korean War veteran who, in his own way, had never stopped fighting. It was his duty, he believed with all his heart, to escort every convicted hood to the slammer and see him appropriately bedded down.

Ironically, no one was more popular around the halls of justice. His wicked wit had somehow endeared him to the judges and to counsel, Crown and defence alike. He was quick to remind confidants that he bore the same Christian name as the then chief justice. The coincidence notwithstanding, no one was more welcome in those lofty chambers than Alfie Wilkes himself.

Kee was up off the chesterfield like a shot. He towered above the little sheriff, grabbed him by the arm and hissed menacingly, "Alfie, if you're putting us on, I'm going to take your head and—"

"You've got a verdict, I told ya," Alfie yelled while shaking off Kee's grip. "Now move it."

Only 35 minutes had passed since Angus had poured the first glass.

Counsel hastily rerobed and were back in the crowded court-room at 3 p.m.

The ceremony remains unchanged.

"All rise," shouted the clerk as the judge was ushered to the dais.

Counsel bowed to the bench.

Faces were solemn, tense.

After the judge was seated, counsel took their places.

"My lady, shall I call the jury?" the clerk asked.

"Please."

The clerk called the jury roll. All were present.

The clerk: "Members of the jury, have you agreed upon your verdict? If so, who shall speak for you?"

"I shall, my lady," the foreman replied.

The juror was recognized by name. Then the critical question:

"Members of the jury, how say you? Do you find the prisoner, John Thomas James Jr., guilty or not guilty?"

Solemnly, the foreman spoke:

"The jury finds the accused, John Thomas James Jr., guilty as charged."

The clerk: "Members of the jury, hearken to your verdict as the court records it. You find John Thomas James Jr. guilty as charged and so say you all?"

"Yes," they nodded and said in unison.

Krindle turned to me. "Are you moving for sentence?"

"I am, my lady."

The clerk to the prisoner: "The prisoner shall rise."

"Mr. James," Krindle began, "you have been convicted by this jury of murder in the first degree. The sentence for that crime is one which is imposed by law. I sentence you to imprisonment for life without parole eligibility for 25 years."

The clerk to the prisoner: "You may sit down."

The ceremony and time-honoured traditions of another trial by jury were over.

Krindle turned away from the prisoner and faced the jurors.

"Members of the jury, may I thank you for the conscientious way in which you have performed your duties during the course of this trial. I appreciate the disruption to your lives in the performance of your civic duty as jurors. You can have the satisfaction of knowing that you have assisted in the orderly and democratic government of our country. I wish to say that you have acted conscientiously and that, in my opinion, the verdict that you have brought in is a reasonable one on the evidence."

She smiled at them graciously.

"Thank you very much. This completes your duties as jurors and you are now discharged."

Seven good women and five good men had reached their verdict after having deliberated for just 3 1/2 hours. They had been chosen by lot to sit in judgment. Their burden had taken its toll. The strain was visible in every face as the 12 citizen judges wordlessly walked out of the jury box.

Counsel rose and bowed to the bench, and the clerk led the judge to her chambers.

Handcuffs snapped around the prisoner's wrists. Sheriff's officers ushered him away.

For most battle-weary lawyers, the verdict brings an end to personal hostilities. They may fight again, but, during the armistice, there are gestures of mutual respect. This day there were none.

I had always saluted my adversary at the end of a trial, often with a hug and never with less than a warm handshake. We had done as adversaries do in law; we had striven mightily, but, again, we would not eat and drink as friends. There were no hands extended nor were there words exchanged.

Silently, we went our separate ways.

Counsel, the more successful ones anyway, skilfully rehearse their witnesses before the day of trial. For the resolute Kee, however, this case required more than good coaching and a couple of practices if John James was to be nailed.

Selflessly, hour after hour, and with tenderness and sympathetic understanding, he talked with Kim, Shirley and Tania. He guided them and nurtured them for their ordeal in the courtroom, and he had become their friend.

After the verdict was pronounced, Kim followed the husky young prosecutor. She caught up to him and waylaid him in a corridor. Her small, white hands reached up and touched his face. She managed to smile, even though tears cascaded down her pale cheeks, and then she embraced him. Almost inaudibly, she whispered, "Thank you." And then she disappeared.

This was an encounter that Kee would always remember. It was, for him, one of life's more rewarding and precious moments.

I stepped into the crowded hallway. Many of the regulars were there. There were handshakes and words of transitory praise. So often I had relished these moments of triumph. But now my spirits were dejected. Despite the verdict, I felt defeated and very tired.

Keyser was speaking with a handful of reporters who had clustered round her. When I passed by, they quickly broke rank and scurried after me.

"What did you think of the verdict, sir?" an apple-cheeked youngster asked earnestly.

"Ms. Keyser says she has a long list of grounds of appeal. Can we have your comments?" asked the pretty girl in the blue denim suit who always smelled of peppermint Lifesavers.

I attempted a friendly smile, said that I would prefer to make no comment, and headed for the stairway.

I stopped on the first landing and removed a pipe from my briefcase. I was surprised to see that my hands shook as I filled the bowl. I sat down on a step, consciously aware that I was physically and emotionally drained.

Even in my sunset years, I had faced each trial with cheerful optimism. Neither unfavourable verdict nor cantankerous judge or lawyer had been able to dampen my enthusiasm—not until the case of Her Majesty the Queen versus John Thomas James Jr.

And now, there appeared through the blue smoke that billowed before my eyes, the beautiful face of the golden-haired child whose days were so short-lived. The pain was very real and it intensified as I remembered the perpetual sorrow I saw in Kim's face.

I thought about the convicted murderer, but could feel no satisfaction. Guilty verdicts do not bring with them the resurrection of the dead.

I reflected bitterly on the ritualistic murder trial, so heavily laced with countless rules and decisions, weighted so disproportionately in favour of the presumably innocent accused. How we cherish and safeguard the rights of the killer. What bloody, naïve , soft-headed fools we are.

Gradually my anger abated. I had done my job. I was, after all, a public prosecutor, not an executioner.

Wearily I got up off the step, picked up my briefcase and clumped down two flights of stairs en route to a preordained rendezvous in my office with five decent men.

When I emerged by a side door, I saw Keyser standing resolutely before a bank of television cameras on the concrete apron at the main entrance to the new Law Courts Building. I cut across Kennedy Street sluggishly and away from the sight of another artless press conference.

As I turned onto Broadway, I wondered what had happened to our once-proud, ancient and honourable profession. What were we now, just a bunch of "rent-a-mouths"?

This should have been an hour for jubilation. It had been a tough murder trial and the killer had been convicted. And yet so many things were beginning to rankle.

Why doesn't the law society tie a can to this free advertising, this blatant display of egotism, this narcissism? I fumed to myself.

It was happening again, another fanciful flight back into my hallucinatory golden era where every advocate was an example of moral rectitude.

There they were. I saw them clearly, those who had earned their great reputations. And where? In the proper forum. In the courtroom!

There was Harry Walsh, who persuaded jurors with impassioned eloquence and logic. A.S. Dewar and D.M. Peden, who confined their superb forensic skills to the four walls of the courtroom. They, and so many others, did not and would not fight their battles in the media. They were the real professionals.

During my post-verdict hour of brooding, my office had undergone a most remarkable transformation. It had become a quasi-cocktail bar, crowded beer room and raucous meeting hall for the policemen and prosecutors who had a vested interest in the fate of John Thomas James Jr.

Five genial hosts, Preisentanz, Gove, Kee, Anderson and

Osborne, scurried about, welcoming the new arrivals and keeping their glasses filled.

They were pleased to take credit for the rapid renovations and hastily compiled guest list. All of them were, however, too generous of spirit to admit that they had paid for the never-ending flow of the best liquor available.

Countless stalwarts came and went. A thousand war stories were retold.

A total abstainer, I found a place to sit on the floor and fell asleep. I was awakened at 10:30 p.m. by Preisentanz, who announced, in a booming voice that could be heard up on the fifteenth floor, that he was hungry.

Kennedy Street is one-way for southbound traffic, and yet two sergeants, a detective and two prosecutors, one an ex-cop, marched north up the centre lane, totally oblivious to the perils of the roadway.

We broke bread together at Tony Roma's restaurant.

These are the precious hours, I told myself. And these are the guys who make it all worthwhile.

The smell of spring was in the air as I wandered down the crescent early the following morning.

A creature of habit, I travelled my usual route with my customary plastic bag of bread crumbs for the sparrows that flock beneath the eaves of old Saint Luke's Parish Church. I paused and listened to their joyful chorus.

And then north I dawdled. One of the kindly sisters waved to me as she entered the door of Holy Rosary Church, a dear soul who would never forsake her faith in man's eternal goodness.

Yesterday's melancholy had passed. It was a new day and there were other battles to be fought.

I picked up the two morning newspapers and stopped off at the Country Style Donuts Shop.

Trial lawyers, being the actors they are, usually study the press accounts of their performances, as I did over a steaming cup of coffee.

"James, 17," I read, "threw his head back against the wall and clenched his eyes shut as Madam Justice Ruth Krindle told the jury she thought they had reached a reasonable verdict. He stood shaking and holding his breath to fight back tears as Krindle told him he'd have no hope of parole for 25 years."[1]

Bob Cox, writing in the other journal, approached the killer's reaction to his fate in these terms:

"John T. James Jr. fought back tears yesterday as he was found guilty of murder and sentenced to spend at least 25 years behind bars. James, freed by a judge on the same charge 52 days ago, threw back his head, looked at the ceiling and then buried his head in his hands as the jury foreman told a packed courtroom of the guilty verdict shortly after 3 p.m."[2]

As I munched on a muffin, my mind reverted to what I had perceived to have been the golden era of journalism, to a time when there were still a few truly worthy of membership in the fourth estate. Take Les Rutherford, for example. For Les, the prisoner's physical and emotional reaction at the moment the verdict was pronounced would be of little concern to his readers. So why bore them? His focus was always on the gravity of the crime and its impact on the victim's loved ones.

Keyser was reported to have said her client was disappointed in the verdict but wanted to appeal immediately.

"He was hoping for the best, but we had told him if there was any ground for appeal, we'd appeal immediately," she said, adding that she "already had a long list of grounds of appeal."

I became irritated. Why not just quietly file a notice of appeal then? Why tell the world about it?

Keyser told reporters her client would likely remain in custody in the Remand Centre until his appeal was filed, then be sent to a maximum security prison at Prince Albert.

Asked if she feared for his safety, Keyser replied, "Not any more than I have all along. I don't think the situation has changed that much."

I neared the southern approaches to the bridge that crosses the winding Assiniboine River and began, curiously enough, to think about Papageno in *The Magic Flute*, a bizarre fellow with peacock feathers on his head, a talkative creature who had to be suppressed. And so the lovely ladies who attended upon the "Queen of the Night" sealed his lips with a padlock.

It is extremely unlikely that Wolfgang Amadeus Mozart was contemplating lawyers when he wrote the opera. Nevertheless, as I whistled my way through a difficult aria, I concluded that, with more padlocks on lawyers' mouths, the world would be a better place.

And so it was on that splendid spring morning, I whistled my way over the river and down the wide boulevard to the majestic old building that houses the courts of justice.

CHAPTER 14

The Appeal

Twenty-eight days after James's conviction for murder, his notice of appeal was filed in the office of the registrar of the Court
of Appeal, the province's highest court.

The first ground of appeal was the standard, colourless, un-
imaginative one—that the said conviction was contrary to the
law, the evidence and the weight of evidence.

Keyser contended secondly that the learned trial judge had
erred in admitting into evidence statements made by the appellant to investigating police officers.

Finally, it was asserted that the trial judge had erred in not
directing the jury to bring back a verdict of acquittal on the charge
of first degree murder.

Later on, the notice was amended by the addition of two
further grounds, among the an allegation that the trial judge
had failed to put the theory of the defence fully and fairly to the
jury.

James was convicted in the early spring. The long hot days
of summer passed, as did the shorter days of autumn. Now winter had come. Almost seven months after the jury had returned
its guilty verdict, Madam Justice Krindle's charge was about to
be microscopically examined by the justices of appeal.

Thursday, November 27, 1986

The Honourable Gordon C. Hall led the panel of judges who, like mourners, filed into the Court of Appeal and slowly sank down into their high-backed, exquisitely carved judicial thrones.

Their robes are black, vestments befitting their funereal faces.

The judges of the trial division dress differently. A wide crimson sash is draped across the right shoulder and down the front of the robe. Ample, elongated French cuffs further adorn their lordly plumage.

Trial judges seem to move faster than those higher up on the judicial ladder. One of them virtually hops up onto the bench and is affectionately known in this jurisdiction as "the Rabbit."

Members of the trial division are prone to smile more frequently, in court at least, than those who are clothed in the more sombre habit.

Gordon Hall was an imposing figure. He was once described by a pert female journalist as a guy who could have easily become one of Hollywood's leading men, another Cary Grant or Ronald Coleman. The square-jawed, blue-eyed World War II paratrooper was in a foul mood.

He was flanked by justices Joseph Francis O'Sullivan and Charles Huband.

If crabbiness were to become the criterion for judicial excellence, then counsel would have found themselves before a most venerable court that morning.

Not so long ago, it had been the court of the genteel jurists, the court of Samuel Freedman, Brian Dickson, Roy Matas and the beloved R.D. "Doc" Guy; a court renowned for its wit, wisdom and civility; a court where delicate humour, employed with tact, was never discouraged.

The litigants and their counsel, the victors and the vanquished, the winners and the losers in the court of the genteel jurists were always in agreement on two counts: they had been heard and they had been treated with respect.

163

There were no preliminary pleasantries.

"Appearances," Hall barked.

Counsel identified themselves.

The convicted murderer had chosen not to be in attendance. There was initial reluctance on the part of the judges to proceed in his absence. They conferenced the matter and there was some delay before they reversed their stance.

"Proceed," Hall ordered, unceremoniously.

Keyser stood up. Like most lawyers who appear before appellate courts, she had quickly learned the magic formula. "With the greatest of respect to the learned trial judge" is a phrase that must precede the artfully constructed judicial insults to follow. Then, and usually with complete impunity, the trial judge is castigated without mercy and every ruling and decision that he or she has made is tediously impeached.

Keyser came quickly to the point. With the greatest of respect to Krindle, she had grievously erred in permitting the jury to hear the statements James had made to the police officers.

When the transparent protestations of respect for the trial judge were excised from Keyser's submission, and when the shameless tendency to euphemize by contending that Krindle had erred was blotted out, what counsel was actually saying was that the trial judge had really screwed up.

Keyser had been on her feet but a short time when the court, collectively, began to fidget. She was interrupted by the senior member.

"What relief are you seeking? What is it you are really asking us to do?" Hall asked wryly.

"To allow the appeal," Keyser replied.

A look of complete incredulity marred his excellent features.

"You are asking us to acquit your client?"

"Yes, my lord."

She reiterated her position. If the court agreed with her contention that John James's statements had been erroneously admitted, then there would be insufficient evidence to sustain her client's conviction.

"You're living in a land of fairy-tales," Hall chortled. And then, completely out of character, the three judges began to laugh.

Bob Cox, writing in the city's largest daily, captured the momentary mood of merriment. "Murder Acquittal Request Prompts Judges' Chuckles," his story was headlined.[1]

After the unexpected laughter had subsided, Keyser resumed her argument with her usual perseverance.

Crown counsel decided to say very little and to rely instead on the filed written argument.

Court was told the Crown found without merit Keyser's allegation that the theory of the defence had not been put to the jury fully and fairly. Further, the trial judge had indeed properly instructed the jury. The verdict of murder in the first degree was the only possible one in light of all of the evidence.

Counsel's tone of voice, like that of his adversary, also expressed true feelings—Ruth Krindle could do no wrong.

The justices agreed among themselves that there appeared to be problems with the trial judge's rulings on the admissibility of James's statements.

Judgment was reserved.

And then they rose and again, like mourners, slowly filed out of the court.

The Christmas season was just around the corner. Soon, the thoughts of men of goodwill everywhere would turn to the wondrous birth of a child in a lowly stable. As for the three judges, their thoughts would return again and again to the tragic death of a child on the floor of a garage. They would miss much of the joy of the festive season as they pondered the killing. There would be countless hours of toil consumed in the preparation of their judgments which they were anxious to deliver early in the new year.

CHAPTER 15

Friday, January 16, 1987

It was mid-afternoon. Kee charged through the office doorway, wildly waving a fistful of paper.

"One day these guys will stand before the judgment seat," he growled as he slumped into a chair. He handed a copy of the decision on the John James appeal across my desk.

All traces of amusement over Kee's dramatic entry quickly vanished as I digested the contents of the first page.

Huband had ordered a new trial. O'Sullivan concurred. Hall had dissented. The majority rules.

"Which guys will stand before the judgment seat one day, Les?" I wanted to know.

"Joe and Charlie," he muttered as he shut the door behind him.

I retired that evening to my book-lined study, a comfortable room that housed, among other indulgences, five pipe racks, two cigar humidors and five tobacco jars—three crafted in rich walnut, two of flawless porcelain.

There was great comfort to be found in this aromatic sanctuary, a refuge from lawyers and thieves, and a haven from "No Smoking" signs.

I selected a briar from a pipe rack on a nearby table.

In the classic work *Nicotiana Tabacum*, a discerning man said: "Light. Then suck in the smoke. Thus your mind will always be lucid and your soul at rest."

Clouds of blue smoke spiralled from the four-square bowl and wreathed around my head as I reached for the copy of the judgment. It was time to discover what mistakes had been made and the means of avoiding them next time.

"The accused," Huband wrote, "was convicted of first degree murder with respect to the death of Ruby Adriaenssens, a three-year-old child. The evidence indicated injury to the child consistent with a sexual assault contemporaneously with the killing. The accused appeals his conviction."

I paused to consider the pasteurized prose, the antiseptic words, so factual and unemotional.

Huband was perhaps one of the three most articulate men in the entire appellate and trial divisions; a man who selected his words carefully and spoke with grace and flare; a former university debating champion, law teacher and barrister who was at home behind the lectern and in the courtroom; a one-time provincial leader of the opposition who was comfortable on the public platform.

I wondered what had happened to him. He was writing about a brutal and sadistic killer, yet the document read like a hospital chart hooked to a patient's bed. The least he could have done was started, "This was a bloody savage murder."

I checked myself and resolved to read dispassionately.

"There was some evidence," Huband wrote, "apart from the accused's confessions, pointing to the accused as the killer. He was seen in the apartment building where the child resided a short time before the child disappeared. The accused then went to a nearby hotel beer parlour to drink with friends in the early evening. He left the hotel alone shortly after 8 p.m. He arrived back at his residence at about 9:30 p.m. The child was noticed to be missing between eight and 9 p.m. In short, the accused was in the vicinity and had the opportunity.

"The child was found the following morning in a garage. The child had been killed by blows to the head by a blunt instrument. A cinder block was found in the garage with blood on it.

"Police investigators found several scalp hairs at the scene of the crime consistent with the scalp hairs of the accused. They found fibres adhering to the clothing of the child which were consistent with the type of fibres in clothing owned by the accused which he might have been wearing that evening.

"However, the convincing evidence that tied the accused with the murder of the little girl came in the form of statements by the accused to police authorities."

Huband recounted the chronology of statements made by James prior to and after he was formally arrested and warned.

"Because the accused was 17 years of age, he is entitled to the benefit of the Young Offenders Act which imposes certain rules governing the admissibility of oral or written statements given by a young person to a person in authority.

"The crucial question for the learned trial judge relating to these various statements was whether some or all of the statements were admissible. The learned trial judge ruled that the exculpatory statement and the confession made by the accused immediately before his arrest, the warnings, and the advice as to the right to counsel were admissible. She ruled that the detailed confession, which followed after the accused's interview with counsel, and the evidence as to what transpired at the scene of the murder were not admissible.

"With the greatest respect, I think the learned trial judge was wrong on all counts. In my view, the exculpatory statement and the first confession are inadmissible while the detailed confession and the evidence as to what transpired at the murder scene constitute admissible evidence.

"I do not mean to be overly critical of the learned trial judge. The ruling on the admissibility of the various statements was made without the luxury enjoyed by an appeal court to consider the arguments and the legal authorities at a leisurely pace."

The majority, in short, had decided that Krindle had admitted those things which she ought not to have admitted, and she had rejected those things which she ought not to have rejected. There would be no absolution for her. Still, she might find comfort in the expression of sensitive understanding of the pressures under which she laboured.

The justice of appeal proffered further balm of Gilead by observing "that the learned trial judge seemed to conclude that those statements which she had rejected were probably admissible but, attempting to err on the side of fairness to the accused, she had excluded them out of an abundance of caution."

The three walnut tobacco jars were packed with my favourite blends—Pirate's Passion, laced with spicy perique; Black Robe, exuding its own rare incense; and Whispering Wind, mild and gentle.

A darkening mood that Friday compelled me to make a symbolic gesture. I selected a squat Peterson Bulldog and filled the bowl. The match ignited the Black Robe and it burned brightly and evenly.

The most celebrated of men have been liable to hallucinations without their conduct offering any sign of mental alienation. And so, in my self-induced hallucinatory state, I puffed away with diabolical satisfaction as the Black Robe went up in smoke. I had burned a judge in effigy.

It had taken a long time to get through the first page and a half of the judgment. I kept going back over what was so self-evident but hadn't quite sunk in.

Clearly, Huband had exonerated Krindle up to a point. But what of the police? Why couldn't another paragraph have magically popped out? How exhilarating to have read:

"I do not wish to be overly critical of the police officers who took the statements from the accused. I appreciate full well the pressures they are under when questioning a murder suspect. They are not afforded the luxury enjoyed by those of us in the appeal court in framing their questions at a leisurely pace."

Saturday, January 17

A new day. I was awakened by healthy hunger pangs and the smell of freshly brewed coffee. To my amazement, I had slept late, a deep, uncluttered sleep.

The non-productive performance of the past evening was history.

Two justices of the province's highest court had found sufficient error to warrant a new trial. Obviously, there were errors, and I meant to learn just what they were. Trials are expensive. They cost the taxpayer plenty. There would be no costly errors when John James came before the court the next time.

I started to read where I had left off.

"The first exculpatory statement was made by the accused to police officers in the early evening of September 14, 1985, approximately one full day after the murder had taken place," Huband wrote.

He recounted the circumstances of James's interviews by Gove and Preisentanz and subsequently by Anderson and Osborne, then he summarized Krindle's ruling on the admissibility of the statements.

"The learned trial judge ruled that all of the comments made by the accused to the police officers, up to the time of the accused's exercising his right to counsel, were admissible. She found as a fact that all of the comments were voluntary. She concluded that, until the accused blurted out that he had grabbed the child and taken her to a garage down the lane, the accused was merely a witness and not a suspect. She concluded that, until an individual becomes a suspect, there is no obligation to give the usual police warnings or advise the witness of the Canadian Charter of Rights and Freedoms' rights to a lawyer. Similarly, she held that a section [Section 56, the full text of which appears in Appendix 2] of the Young Offenders Act did not apply until such time as the accused became a suspect rather than a witness. The difficulty in this case focuses on this latter point.

"The Young Offenders Act makes no distinction between a statement of a person who is seen to be a witness as opposed to one who is regarded as a suspect. The section simply states that 'a statement…given by a young person…to a person in authority…' is not admissible unless certain criteria are met. The first criteria is that the statement is voluntary, and the learned trial judge correctly found that both the exculpatory statement and the inculpatory statement made by the accused immediately prior to the police warnings met this requirement.

"The remaining criteria under the section were not met. Up to that point, the accused was not told that he was under no obligation to give a statement. He was not told that any statement given by him might be used as evidence in proceedings against him. He was not advised of his right to consult with counsel, a parent, or an adult relative. He was not given the opportunity to make his statements in the presence of counsel, a parent, or an adult relative of his choice."

I pondered the implications of this interpretation. The Young Offenders Act, then, makes no distinction between a statement of a person who is seen to be a witness and one who is regarded as a suspect. I adopted Mr. Bumble's words as my own: "If the law supposes that, the law is a ass, a idiot."[2]

I was starting to regress again, so I quickly turned away from Charles Dickens and back to Charles Huband.

"These criteria," the judge wrote, "have no application with respect to an oral statement made spontaneously before there is a reasonable opportunity to comply with the requirements. It was not seriously argued either before the learned trial judge or in this court that the statements were made 'spontaneously.' The accused had been in police headquarters for interrogation for in excess of four hours. The statements had been elicited from him through a series of interviews conducted by two teams of police officers. As the evening progressed, it became apparent that the accused was dissembling, and the police officers were striving for further information and clarification. The accused was being pressed to answer the questions. No doubt the confession that he had grabbed the child and taken her to a garage came as a surprise to the investigating officers, but it can hardly be called 'spontaneous.'"

I went over the preceding paragraph again, my eyes focusing on the word "dissembling." Why didn't the judge just say that James was bullshitting the police?

I paused to question not only my vulgarity, but also the cynicism and anger that would not go away. The very thought of a new trial for the killer in the wake of the jury's unanimous verdict was gnawing at me like a bleeding ulcer. I tossed the judgment across the room. Many weeks would pass before I could return to it.

Sunday, January 18

Inevitably following the Court of Appeal decision, there would be post-mortems in the press, along with the irrepressible defence counsel's commentaries.

Keen neophyte reporters with a misguided sense of duty scampered off to get the reaction of members of the victim's family, oblivious in their zeal to the right of the poor bereaved souls to some peace and privacy. Once the plaintive little stories were written, editors predictably constructed what they perceived to be poignant headlines.

Large, black, block capitals needlessly announced self-evident truths. "RUBY'S MOM IS SHOCKED BY RULING" declared one daily newspaper.[3] "NEW TRIAL NIGHTMARE FOR FAMILY" stated another.[4]

Kim Adriaenssens was too upset to speak to journalists. It was left to her mother, Shirley, to express the family's distress at the fact that James would be retried.

"He's confessed twice; what more do they want?" she was quoted as asking in one article. "Why is this continuing?"

A reporter contacted Samay Suvannasorn, who had discovered Ruby's body. His garage had become such a gruesome reminder of the horror that he tore the building down five days after the terrible experience. But the painful memory of the child could never be demolished. It was indelibly etched in Samay's brain. Understandably, he did not want to testify again.

"I don't want to get involved anymore," he said. "I'd rather forget it."

Among Brenda Keyser's public offerings was a suggestion that it would be hard to find a fair and impartial jury for a second trial since the case had gained so much media coverage.

"I think everyone from here to Tuktoyaktuk has heard of the case because of the media coverage," she commented.

If so, I thought caustically, it was with a fair amount of assistance from yourself.

Keyser also said that a new trial judge would not have to follow the higher court's decision about the admissibility of James's second confession.

"It's obviously a strong comment to the court below," she claimed, "but it's something that can be worked around."

I shuffled over to a bookcase and removed Mark M. Orkin's *Legal Ethics: A Study of Professional Conduct*, published in 1957.

Orkin would have been greatly distressed by the ever-increasing, indiscriminate manipulation of the media, electronic and print, by those practitioners who seem hell-bent on bringing the legal profession into further disrepute.

In his chapter on "Solicitation of Business," the learned author commented on newspaper interviews. He wrote:

"Indirect advertisement for business by furnishing or inspiring newspaper comment concerning causes in which the lawyer has been or is connected, or concerning the manner of their conduct, the magnitude of the interests involved, the importance of the lawyer's position, and like self-laudations defy the traditions and lower the tone of the lawyers' high calling, and should not be tolerated."[5]

The reasoning behind this sentence of the canon is obvious. If it is unprofessional to advertise directly, it is equally improper to do so indirectly. As Chief Justice Mathers said:

"The discussion of causes, in which the lawyers may be retained, in the newspaper, the unfolding of the particular line of attack or defence which they propose to adopt, is most unbecoming. The lawyer who has a regard for professional propriety will refrain from such meretricious publicity."[6]

My wife had thoughtfully prepared a mug of Postum. As I sipped, I began to mellow.

Perhaps inadvertently, perhaps not, my indulgent spouse had selected one of my most cherished mugs, the one inscribed with the sixth King Henry's noble aspiration to do first things first—to kill all the lawyers. And secondly, I thought, let's kill all the newspaper reporters.

The Huband Judgment Revisited

Blessed is the man who gets well paid for his hobby.

I tenderly withdrew a new volume of the *Canadian Criminal Cases* from its cardboard moorings. These are works of non-fiction, crammed with stories of real people, their successes and failures, their loves and hates, stories of lust and greed; a constant source of adventure, romance, intrigue and plenty of gruesome homicides for the murder-mystery buff, as well.

The trick was to read these books selectively, savouring the factual situations while skimming the legal discourses. "Reading law" in my own narrow field was good entertainment. There was an added bonus, too. Frequently I would recall a useful word, phrase or passage that could be used now and again most effectively in court.

Sometimes a page in a reported decision would glow with an aura of warmth and understanding and compassion as if it had been lifted from the soul of a Chaim Potok novel.

Another Saturday morning in my den. I took Volume 33 of the *Canadian Criminal Cases (New Series)* from a shelf, turned to page 247 and found the place in the Huband judgment where I had given up a couple of months earlier. The cynicism, I hoped, had taken wing, but I read with as much enthusiasm as if I were poring over one of last year's seed catalogues.

Referring to the Young Offenders Act, Huband wrote that:

"Under S-S.(4) of S.56, the requirements of S.56(2)B) and (C) may be waived. In this case the police requested that the accused sign a document waiving these requirements, but he refused to do so."

The act, then, provides that a "young person" may waive his right, before he makes a statement, to consult with counsel, a parent or an adult relative. However, such waiver shall be made in writing and shall contain a statement signed by the young person in which he acknowledges that he has been apprised of the right that he is waiving. If such consultation does in fact take place, the young person may waive his right to make a statement in the presence of such person, providing the waiver is in writing.

"Crown counsel," Huband went on, "argues that the learned trial judge was right in concluding that Section 56 does not apply to a witness as opposed to a suspect. Were it not so, it was argued, then in every investigation of a crime where a young person is interviewed, it would be necessary to give the usual police warnings and advice as to the right to counsel, simply to obtain a statement from a witness. Not so. Police authorities will continue to interview witnesses, adult or otherwise, without these preliminaries. Where the witness is not himself involved in criminal activities, there will be no need to give warnings and invite consultation with legal counsel. In those rare instances where the witness is involved in criminal activities, and where the statements might prove useful evidence against him, then the police must obtain a waiver under S-S.(4), or, if that is not available, obtain a further statement after the criteria in Section 56(2)B), (C) and (D) have been met.

"In the instant case, the police tried without success to obtain a waiver, and consequently the statements which do not meet the criteria set forth in Section 56 are not admissible against the accused.

"On the other hand, it would seem to me, on the record before the learned trial judge, that the later statements, which are highly incriminating, were voluntary and were obtained after compliance with Section 56. When it became clear that the accused was the likely killer, the police gave him the usual police warnings and advised him of his right to counsel. The accused exercised his right to counsel, and his lawyer attended at the Public Safety Building on Sunday, September 15th, at 12:15 a.m. She was allowed to proceed with an interview with the accused commencing at 12:32 a.m....

"At 1:45 a.m., officers Anderson and Osborne reattended upon the accused.... Having obtained the required background information, Constable Osborne then invited the accused to make a written statement about what had happened. The accused refused because of his lawyer's advice. But the discussion with the police officers continued...."

It was then, Huband recounted, that the accused acknowledged he had gone back to the Inglis Block from the Maryland Hotel and had taken Ruby, sexually attacked her, and struck her twice with a concrete block. While being transported to the Manitoba Youth Centre, the accused subsequently made further statements to the police as they approached and viewed the murder scene.

"On the *voir dire* hearing," Huband wrote, "the learned trial judge concluded that the statements made by the accused to the police at the Public Safety Building, after having consulted with his lawyer, and later when he retraced his route at the scene of the crime, were voluntary in nature. All of these statements came after he had been told that he need not say anything, but that anything that he did say might be used as evidence against him. He had been told of his right to counsel, and had exercised that right.

"Under Section 56, any statement made by the young person is required to be made in the presence of legal counsel, with whom the accused had consulted, unless the young person desires otherwise. In this case, legal counsel attended upon the accused. Thereafter, the accused refused to give a written statement but proceeded to answer police questions. The accused had full opportunity to make a statement in the presence of his legal counsel but obviously chose not to do so when she was present at the Public Safety Building. By volunteering information after she had left, I think it is clear that, by his own choice, he responded to the questions without his lawyer being present. We know nothing of what took place in the interview between the accused and legal counsel, but one might reasonably infer that the accused was advised of his rights, including the right to maintain his silence, or alternatively, if he were to give a statement, to make that statement in the presence of his legal counsel. Legal counsel was present at the Public Safety Building, and if the accused had wished to make a statement in the presence of his counsel, it could have been done then. He was afforded the right to make a statement in the presence of counsel and chose not to do so. He volunteered a statement after his counsel had departed."

Huband cited examples in case law where statements made by accused persons after they had been closeted with counsel and cautioned were deemed admissible. The test, it was noted, was whether the statements were voluntary in the sense that they were not made from fear or prejudice, or from hope of advantage.

In reference to the James case, the judge continued:

"When the accused was taken to the apartment building and was asked to retrace the route that he had followed with the child when the crime was committed, once again, the accused voluntarily answered police questions. It seems to me that the questions and answers were admissible. But even if they were not, I think that the police officers could testify that, in response to their request, the accused showed them the route that he had followed with the child, showed them the garage where the crime had been committed, and showed them the weapon used to kill the child.

"In the present case, the physical evidence as to what occurred at the scene of the crime, when the accused showed the police officers what he had done, constitutes 'admissible evidence.'"

Dejectedly, I read the close of the judgment.

"In my opinion, the result of this appeal must be a new trial.

Evidence which was crucial in the conviction of the accused is inadmissible. Without that evidence (and without the evidence which was strongly excluded by the learned trial judge) the case against the accused is not a strong one.

"It is not for this court to weigh the evidence, which the learned trial judge wrongly excluded, in order to maintain the conviction. That evidence was not put before the jury. It is for a jury to consider and weigh that evidence, and make a determination as to the guilt of the accused accordingly."

The Hall Dissent

More well-worn words.

"I have had," Hall began, "the advantage of reading the reasons for judgment of my brother Huband."

Why, for once, couldn't a dissent commence: "There was no advantage whatsoever in my having read the reasons for judgment fumbled by my brothers in the majority"?

Hall went on:

"I agree with him, and for the reasons which he gives, that evidence was excluded which should have been admitted, and that evidence was admitted which should have been excluded. However, I cannot agree that a new trial is appropriate because, but for the impugned evidence, the case is not a strong one. In my opinion, the case against the accused is a strong one.

"As pointed out by my brother Huband, the accused was in the vicinity and had the opportunity to commit the crime. The scalp hairs and fibres found at the scene are strong inferential facts pointing to the guilt of the accused. A cinder block with blood on it was found at the scene. The evidence excluded, which should have been admitted, where the accused pointed out to the police officers the route he took, the garage where the murder took place and the cinder block which was used is virtually unimpeachable and could not be open to serious attack on a new trial. That evidence was before the court on the *voir dire* leading to its exclusion and was not impugned."

An appellate court has many powers, including the power to dismiss an appeal in appropriate circumstances. It may dismiss the appeal where, notwithstanding that there has been a wrong decision on a question of law, the court is of the opinion that no substantial wrong or miscarriage of justice has occurred.

Clearly, Hall had based his decision on an application of that curative provision. He was not unmindful, he stressed, of the care which must be taken in invoking the "no miscarriage of justice" provision of the Criminal Code.

"It does seem to me," he wrote, "at the end of the day that the admissible evidence makes out a strong case against the accused and that the jury would not, as reasonable persons, have done otherwise than to have found the accused guilty.

"Another point. My brother Huband says that it is not for this court to weigh the evidence which was wrongly excluded, because that is for a jury on a new trial. If that would be a serious exercise for the jury, I would agree; but is it? In my opinion, highly unlikely. What the accused pointed out to the police officers, as previously mentioned, cannot seriously be doubted.

"One final observation, leaving aside the evidence admitted in error, I feel constrained to say that many an accused has been convicted and the case affirmed on appeal on much less inferential facts than here present."

Hall concluded that he would invoke the "no miscarriage" provision and dismiss the appeal.

So would I.

CHAPTER 16

The Second Trial:
Tuesday, April 21, 1987

By 9:40 a.m., many of the "regulars" at the first trial had planted themselves in the chairs that they would occupy, by squatter sovereignty, for the duration of the second trial.

The would-be Thespians who devour the drama of the courtroom were among them. Others who, but for the grace of God, might have become lawyers also were in their customary places. (To share a word or exchange a nod with the counsel of their choice seems to make their day.)

Courtroom buffs are a rare species. They conduct themselves, for the most part, as if they were in a consecrated place. If one of them has to communicate with a fellow squatter, he does so self-consciously and with great restraint.

For them, the courtroom, like the sanctuary, is hallowed ground, a place of quietude.

"All rise," shrieked the needle-nosed, bespectacled clerk as the clock struck 10 a.m. She had shattered the tranquillity and the steely-eyed gaze of the squatters was upon her.

All rose but for Kenny Tacium, who couldn't. He sat at the Crown counsel table, his white-knuckled hands gripping the arms of his wheelchair as Chief Justice Benjamin Hewak of the Court of Queen's Bench strode into the courtroom and onto the dais.

This was supposed to have been a heady moment for the

young barrister who had fantasized about becoming a lion in court. All Tacium could feel, however, was a gnawing at his entrails and an abiding conviction that he should have stayed in by-law court.

Les Kee had been at him for weeks.

"Kenny, you've got to hustle your ass down to Malabar's and pick up your gown by this weekend," he implored. "We're starting on Monday."

The fledgling sat dejectedly, bemoaning his attendance at the legal robe-maker's and contemplating a premature interment. He tugged on his new barrister's gown and hitched it higher around his neck, hoping that his ghostly pallor would be hidden in the raven-black folds.

Tacium had served under articles in the attorney general's department and, as a student, had prepared two lengthy briefs for us prior to the first James murder trial.

It was Kee who had pressured for Tacium's participation in court. It was an opportunity for the newcomer to get some experience guiding minor Crown witnesses through their evidence.

"So what if it is murder one?" Kee persisted. "I've got confidence in the kid."

Apart from Tacium's addition to the prosecution team, the same players dressed for the second match—Brenda Keyser and Drew Baragar for the defence, myself and Kee for the Crown.

A weird assortment of shapes and sizes, encased in the uncomfortable, archaic black robes that must be worn in the higher courts, bowed in unison to the bench.

"Mr. Kenneth Tacium is with Mr. Kee and I, my lord, and will take an active part in this prosecution," I informed the presiding judge.

Kenny leaned forward in his wheelchair and lowered his head in deference to the broad-shouldered figure seated upon his judicial throne high atop Mount Olympus. The chief justice, who was built like a Chicago Bears corner linebacker, looked down at the frail and timorous young lawyer and studied him intently.

Kenny confided later that, during this brief interval of

scrutiny, he had strained himself to the limit to maintain dominion over his sphincter. At that very moment, Kee gently draped his big left arm around Tacium's shoulders.

Hewak's words of welcome were terse, but the penetrating judicial eye and broad smile on the face of one for whom laughter was a semi-annual event (in court at least) conveyed a singular message: 'You'll do just fine in this league, son.'

A tinge of pink spread across the pallid face. Knots in the lower abdomen were loosening. Miraculously, the pangs of fear were subsiding. With the powerfully built jurist up front and the rugged Kee flanking him, Tacium was ready for his forensic baptism.

Kim Adriaenssens had endured 365 sorrow-filled days since Monday, April 21, 1986, when the first jury was selected to try her daughter's murderer. Now, a second jury was about to be selected to retry the killer. This time, however, more than a day was consumed before six men and six women could be duly empanelled and sworn.

Why is it that all things legal must be "duly" delivered, "duly" inscribed or "duly" done? Does the barber "duly" clip the hair and "duly" trim the beard?

In any event, the second trial was now "duly" under way.

Judges, like lawyers, come in a variety of shapes and sizes. The judicial bench upon which the winsome Madam Justice Krindle had been ensconced during James's first murder trial was disproportionately large for her tiny frame. By contrast, Hewak's chair was disproportionately small for his ample body. In his law school days, and afterwards as Crown counsel, he had been known to his intimates as "the Giant Buddha."

By his stature and commanding presence, Hewak personified the awesome dignity and majesty of the law. One might have expected a booming voice, but he spoke softly. His opening remarks, while not dissimilar to those of Krindle, were delivered with a singular lack of animation.

My address was a replay of what I had said to the first jury.

I saw no need to deviate; the same witnesses would be called. There was one conscious variation, however. I must not appear to be sitting in the seat of the scornful, even though I had sat nowhere else since the Court of Appeal had ordered a new trial.

I knew that the prisoner was guilty and I intended to prove it, but this jury must only hear the voice of the impartial prosecutor, the measured tones of a law officer of the Crown who still adhered to the myth that the Crown never wins and the Crown never loses.

Once again, Constable Craig Boan, the first witness for the prosecution, tendered photographs taken at the murder scene. Again, jurors gasped at the sight of the bloodied child. One held her hand over her mouth; another shook her head, then gazed into space, bewildered; yet another's features were wreathed in anger.

Every word from the lips of witness after witness was digested by as attentive a jury as had ever been assembled.

Tania Adriaenssens, now 15, testified on the third day.

At the first trial, she had been asked to cast her mind back to the events of September 13, 1985, 200 days earlier—an eternity in the life of the then 13-year-old. She was expected to recall, accurately, details of the circumstances immediately prior to her niece's abduction, a tall order for anyone, big or little.

Bravely she crossed the crowded courtroom floor past so many staring faces and stood in the witness box before a jury of strangers. She was compelled to relive, once more, the saddest time in her young life, when Ruby went away forever.

Our laggard justice system exacts its toll. With each passing day, most memories become clouded. Unlike the police officer and expert witness, the civilian rarely makes handwritten notes of situations and conversations in anticipation of a need, down the road, to refresh a faulty memory.

Just before Tania was about to testify, she glanced shyly across the courtroom at Kee with anxious eyes. I could have sworn he surreptitiously blew the young lady a kiss. In any event, she smiled and then, in her sweet innocence, told the second jury exactly what she had said before, so long ago.

She was a most remarkable witness with an exceptional memory. Still, it was obvious that Kee had worked long and hard to prepare her for the second trial. She attested to events that happened 585 days earlier. With a mixture of relief and profound admiration, my eyes followed her as she walked away from the witness box.

The cumulative testimony of those witnesses who had known and loved the murdered child visibly moved each juror.

And then came the revelations of the pathologist and pediatrician, uncamouflaged, graphic and raw. The faces of the 12 citizens in the jury box mirrored pain and anguish that were very real as they grappled with this oppressive evidence.

On the fourth day of the trial, Hewak excused the jurors. Then, he listened patiently to the testimony of the investigating officers who questioned James.

There were few interruptions from the bench, but the juristic pen moved non-stop across the pages of his trial book. The judge, unlike counsel, seemed tireless. He laboriously recorded every word in each statement and every comment that James had made to the officers.

When it came time for him to make his rulings on the admissibility of the various statements, he, unlike Krindle, enjoyed a unique advantage. The rulings, subject to insignificant qualifications, had already been made for him by the Court of Appeal.

At 2:05 p.m. on the sixth day of the trial, Hewak addressed counsel in the absence of the jury:

"It is axiomatic in the judicial process that judges of trial divisions are bound by the rulings and decisions of appellate courts. They are bound and obliged to follow such rulings until the ultimate appeal court of the land, that is, the Supreme Court of Canada, delivers decisions that affirm those rulings or correct the errors of both appellate and trial courts. Ultimately, that court determines the proper application and interpretation of the law.

"However, until that happens, the interpretation of the law

given by the appellate courts is supreme, and, in the absence of some distinguishing factual difference, the trial courts are obliged to follow their rulings and findings.

"Such is the situation in this case. In a previous trial of this accused on this charge, the very same issues of admissibility, based on the same grounds and on the same facts, were presented to the learned trial judge, Madam Justice Krindle. The submissions were made on the same type of evidence that had been presented before me on a *voir dire* hearing....

"On the evidence before me in this *voir dire*, I find:

"One: That I am totally satisfied, beyond any reasonable doubt, that any comments or actions by the accused to the police, both before and during their investigation and subsequent to the arrest of the accused, were voluntary. I accept the police evidence at all times when they describe the accused as being polite and co-operative and when they describe their own attitude and behaviour as being professional and controlled.

"Two: That initially, based on the facts presented before me, the accused was not dealt with in accordance with the provisions of Section 56, subsection (2) of the Young Offenders Act. Consequently, following the direction of the Court of Appeal and based on their interpretation and application of the relevant law, I exclude as inadmissible all the statements made to the police by the accused up until the time he asked to consult with counsel.

"Three: Again, following the direction of the Court of Appeal and based upon their interpretation of the relevant law, I find that any statements, actions or comments made by the accused after he was arrested and informed of his rights under the charter and under the Young Offenders Act, particularly after he consulted with his counsel, and with Harry James, his closest adult relative, are admissible in evidence."

I whispered into Tacium's ear: "The Lord giveth and the Lord taketh away. The last confession is in and the first one is out."

The chief justice, following the majority in the appellate division, had decreed that neither Sergeant Preisentanz nor Constable Gove could attest as to John James's exculpatory statement. In other words, the second jury would hear nothing about the nimble-tongued killer's attempt to finger Eli Tacan for the child's murder. And it would hear nothing of James's admission to Sergeant Anderson and Constable Osborne that he had grabbed the little girl and taken her to the garage down the lane.

Yet, the die was cast. The accused's subsequent detailed confession and what he said to the officers at the murder scene constituted admissible evidence.

On the eighth day of the trial, court adjourned at 5:05 p.m. and the jurors began to consider their verdict. They returned at 9:30 p.m.

Guilty as charged!

Predictably, the press apprised its readers of the killer's reaction.

Heidi Graham of the *Winnipeg Free Press* conveyed the sharp-eyed observation that "John James dropped his head to his chest after he was found guilty for the second time of the first degree murder of three-year-old Ruby Adriaenssens."[1]

Linda Williamson of the *Winnipeg Sun*, vying for top honours in journalistic excellence, proffered her tawdry observations:

"James, 18," she wrote, "bowed to the six-man, six-woman jury who found him guilty of first degree murder, then stood tall as he prepared to face life in prison with no hope of parole for 25 years.

"He smiled and shook the hands of his lawyers, Brenda Keyser and Drew Baragar.

"'Nice try,' he said."[2]

CHAPTER 17

"Justice depends in the last analysis on equity, on the concept of fairness. If we can escape from the shackles of technicalities and seek always the equity of the situation, we shall be moving towards justice."
—Chief Justice S. Freedman (1908-1993)

The Second Appeal

"Manners are of more importance than laws," Edmund Burke wrote. "Upon them, in great measure, the laws depend. The law touches us but here and there, and now and then. Manners are what vex or soothe, corrupt or purify, exalt or debase, barbarize or refine us, by a constant, steady, uniform, insensible operation, like that of the air we breathe in."[1]

Good manners were in short supply among those who sat on the province's loftiest bench on Friday morning, December 18, 1987.

But then, most counsel who appeared on a regular basis in that court at that stage in its history had come to realize, to their sorrow, they were no longer in the court of the genteel jurists.

All too frequently, they were interrupted with coarse comments more befitting a barroom than a courtroom. Something lustrous had been tarnished; something sacred, profaned.

Brenda Keyser did not mince words as she bid for a third trial for James.

The incriminating statement, which resulted in large measure in her client's conviction, had been wrongfully obtained, she contended. Anderson and Osborne were the culprits. Their failure to instruct James as to his right to have a lawyer or adult relative present when they questioned him clearly violated the Young Offenders Act. In a nutshell, the trial judge had erred in allowing the jurors to hear the appellant's confession.

A very testy panel of law lords was all over Keyser, figuratively speaking, as she tried to develop her argument. She was met with ceaseless interruptions and caustic comments. In this climate of injudicious hostility, the visitor in the gallery must have been sorely troubled on that December morn.

Keyser conceded that, while police permitted her client to speak to his second cousin and to herself soon after his arrest, they erred in not telling him that he could have an adult relative or lawyer present during the actual questioning.

"If this man was convicted, it's because he didn't understand his counsel," Mr. Justice O'Sullivan snapped. "Counsel didn't make him aware that if he answered any questions, he's going to spend the next 25 years in jail—it's unbelievable."

An equally incredulous Chief Justice Alfred Monnin proclaimed that Keyser's argument was basically an admission that she hadn't done her job by informing James of all of his rights.

"What's the use of lawyers going into a room and not telling the client of his rights?" he asked, adding gratuitously that "there must be a lot of stupid lawyers out there if her argument was true."

Again, O'Sullivan joined the chorus.

"It was your job, not the job of the police, to inform the accused of his rights," he lectured the beleaguered counsel.

Kee and I argued that, even if the police had not adhered with exactitude to the letter of the Young Offenders Act, they had complied with it in spirit; further, there most certainly was additional evidence to sustain the conviction.

The court reserved its decision.

188

"Nobody mentioned little Ruby's rights bloody once," Kee remarked dejectedly as the great oak door closed behind the last departing jurist.

Seven days and it would again be Christmas. But there would be no glad tidings for Kim Adriaenssens and scant comfort and joy.

Friday, January 22, 1988: The Second Huband Judgment

My heart was as cold as the wintry night itself. The appeal court had delivered its judgment in the case of Her Majesty the Queen versus John James Jr. (No. 2).

MANSLAUGHTER!

The court had dismissed the appeal and substituted the lesser verdict of manslaughter for the jury's verdict of murder in the first degree.

I shut my eyes and grimaced as my mind flashed back to another January evening a year ago when I sat in the same chair in my den, trying to comprehend the first appeal court judgment concerning the killer James. Now I had before me another Huband/O'Sullivan bombshell.

Huband began with the obligatory summary of the circumstances of the second appeal, then wrote:

"Without in any way being critical of Chief Justice Hewak, I would observe that in the earlier appeal, this court did not give a 'directive' that the evidence now in dispute must be ruled admissible. An opinion was clearly expressed, but, in the context of the case, it was an *obiter* opinion which I would fully expect the Chief Justice to follow."

I looked up from the page and pondered about some judges who, like most lawyers, have danced too long at the nit-pickers' ball.

"It was my view," Huband continued, "that the statements and actions of the accused subsequent to his arrest and his consultation with legal counsel met the criteria for admissibility set forth in the Young Offenders Act. Upon further reflection and upon hearing the issue fully argued, I conclude that I was wrong in part."

The words of the English author Chesterton came rushing back: "...determining the guilt or innocence of men is a thing too important to be trusted to trained men.... But when it wishes anything done that is really serious, it collects twelve of the ordinary men standing about."

Six ordinary men and six ordinary women did determine the guilt of John James, and they found him guilty of murder in the first degree. Two trained men, Huband and O'Sullivan, overruled them and found him guilty of manslaughter.

I plodded on through yet another skeletal outline of James's interviews with police and his confessions.

"After having had the benefit of meeting with his lawyer," Huband observed, "the accused volunteered answers to questions posed by the police. It might be argued that, having been apprised of his rights, the accused obviously desired to make his statement by way of answers to police questions without the benefit of the presence of legal counsel. That was my earlier impression. But, in the end, that argument cannot be sustained. An explanation must be given to the young person that his legal counsel is required to be present unless the accused makes a conscious choice to proceed with the statement in the absence of his counsel. No such explanation was given, and, as a consequence, the accused made no conscious choice to give his answers in the absence of legal counsel. The provisions...seem to be based on the premise that a young person is more susceptible to suggestion, and more likely to co-operate with persons in authority than an adult offender. Consequently, the statements or confessions of young persons should not be admitted unless these added protections are made available. Even though he enjoyed the benefit of consultation with his lawyer, an explanation must be given to him that his lawyer is to be present while he answers further questions unless he otherwise desires. It cannot be said that, had the explanation been given, the accused would have elected to continue with his answers without his lawyer being recalled. Had the lawyer been recalled, it would seem obvious that the answers would not have been given.

"Concerning the 'reasonable opportunity to make the statement in the presence' of his lawyer, once again I am compelled to conclude that there was non-compliance with the provision. It is true that the accused's lawyer had attended the police station, and had the accused been minded to make a statement, it could have been made while the lawyer was present.

"But it is clear that the accused formed no intention to make a statement during the time that his lawyer was present. Indeed, after she left, the accused told the police that her instructions were that he should not give a written statement. Apparently the accused was under the impression that oral responses to police questions were a different matter. Under the circumstances, I think that the accused was entitled to be told by the police that they would endeavour to recall his lawyer before proceeding with the series of questions and answers.

"Had the accused been an adult, I for one can see nothing about the police investigation which would make inadmissible the incriminating responses.

"When the first appeal from a conviction for murder was considered by this court, I expressed the view that there was compliance with the Young Offenders Act. Upon closer review, I am persuaded that this preliminary view was wrong, and that the answers given by the accused to police questioning from 1:55 a.m. until 2:02 a.m. on September 15, 1985, do not constitute admissible evidence."

During those seven minutes, the killer had told Anderson and Osborne that he had grabbed the child when he saw her walking up the stairs. In the garage, he had tried to penetrate her tiny body, both vaginally and anally. He admitted having struck her with a brick when she screamed out in her torment. He confessed that he thought that he had killed her.

Madam Justice Krindle had "out of an abundance of caution" refused to permit the jury to hear the killer's detailed confession. The Court of Appeal judges said that she had erred. A year later, two of the members of the original panel decided, in reversing themselves, that she had quite properly kept this confession out.

"But that does not end the matter," Huband continued. "Shortly after 3:40 a.m., there was the visit to the scene of the crime....

"[W]hat happened at the time of the visit to the murder site stands independently from the earlier confession. What occurred simply constitutes material facts in the case. It is a material fact that, at around 3:40 a.m. on September 15th, in response to a police officer's question, the accused pointed out the door in the apartment building where the Adriaenssens child resided from which he had exited along with the child. It is a material fact that, pursuant to a police request, the accused proceeded to show the police officers the route that he had taken with the child from the apartment building down a back lane, across a major thoroughfare, and then continuing down the back lane to the garage where the child was found dead. It is a material fact that, in answer to further inquiry, the accused pointed out the spot where the concrete block was located with which the child was killed, and that particular location was consistent with what the police had found in their investigation as a spot where a concrete block had likely been located.

"Perhaps this evidence on its own would not be sufficient to result in a conviction," Huband ventured to observe. "But there was other evidence, quite apart from the confession, pointing towards the guilt of the accused and when that evidence is coupled with the actions and gestures of the accused in response to police questions at the scene of the crime, I am convinced that the guilt of the accused is established beyond all reasonable doubt."

I snatched Volume 33 of the *Canadian Criminal Cases (3rd Series)* from the shelf. There they were in black and white, the words that I was looking for; words that Huband had written just 12 months before:

"Evidence which was crucial in the conviction of the accused is inadmissible. Without that evidence (and without the evidence which was wrongly excluded by the learned trial judge) the case against the accused is not a strong one."

O'Sullivan had concurred in that opinion. Gordon Hall hadn't. He wrote:

"In my opinion, the case against the accused is a strong one."

I returned to my chair, relit my pipe and puffed my way through both trials. The latter was a duplicate of the former minus the testimony of Eli Tacan.

For Huband, the first case against the accused was not a strong one. The second one convinced him of the guilt of the accused, established beyond all reasonable doubt.

"I just don't understand," I muttered out loud.

Comprehension became even more elusive as I proceeded through Huband's detailed exposition of the hair and fibre evidence.

In the earlier judgment, he had devoted but two lines to the vitally significant hair evidence, noting only that "Police investigators found several scalp hairs at the scene of the crime consistent with the scalp hairs of the accused."

This time there were 51 lines on scalp and pubic hairs.

Similarly, Huband previously accorded the potent fibre evidence a measly 3 1/2 lines: "They [the police investigators] found fibres adhering to the clothing of the child which were consistent with the type of fibres in clothing owned by the accused, which he might have been wearing that evening."

One year later, he proclaimed that "The evidence of comparable hairs and fibres is very strong evidence indicating that the accused was indeed in the garage with the Adriaenssens child at the time the killing took place."

The forensic evidence was identical in both of the murder trials. Why then was the first case weak and the second stronger?

Whatever the answer, Huband concluded that the hair and fibre evidence, coupled with the evidence of the visit to the site of the crime, conclusively established the guilt of the accused.

"But guilt as to what crime?" he then asked rhetorically.

The question had arisen during the December 18 appeal

hearing. O'Sullivan had invited counsel to comment on a judgment of the Supreme Court of Canada (R. v. Vaillancourt) delivered 15 days earlier.

Vaillancourt was convicted of murder as a result of the death of a person during an armed robbery in a pool hall. The victim had been shot by Vaillancourt's accomplice. The majority of the Supreme Court concluded that it would violate the Canadian Charter of Rights and Freedoms to allow a conviction for murder without proof of the intent to cause death or proof of the intent to cause bodily harm likely to result in death.

The effect of this decision was to cast doubt on the constitutional validity of the section of the Criminal Code of Canada under which John James had been charged.

Keyser acknowledged she had a copy of the judgment, but told the appeal court she was not relying on it, nor was she prepared to discuss it. The Crown took the same position.

Huband, however, was prepared to refer to it in his written judgment. The Vaillancourt case, he noted, was one of constructive murder that the Supreme Court decided could not stand because of charter violations. The same reasoning, he surmised, would apply in the James case.

Alas, a straightforward murder had become hopelessly entangled in a web of technicalities.

As defined in the Criminal Code of Canada, culpable (blameworthy) homicide is murder where the person who causes the death of a human being

(i) means to cause his death, or

(ii) means to cause him bodily harm that he knows is likely to cause his death and is reckless whether death ensues or not.

"It may well be," Huband wrote, "that the accused would be found guilty of murder under that section of the Criminal Code which defines murder, quite apart from the constructive murder section which deals with death during the commission of a sexual assault.

"One suspects that when the accused struck the child's head with the cinder block, he either meant to cause death or meant to cause bodily harm that he knew was likely to cause death."

Wearily, I turned to the last page.

"If a new trial were ordered, while I think it likely that the accused would be reconvicted of murder under Section..."

I stopped in mid-sentence and stared in pop-eyed disbelief.

"If a new trial were ordered, while I think it likely that the accused would be reconvicted of murder...it is conceivable that the conviction could be for manslaughter rather than murder. Manslaughter, it seems to me, is the best possible result that this accused could expect."

As James had already had two trials for murder, Huband went on to argue, it was in the public interest as well as in the accused's interest that the process be brought to an end.

"I would exercise the authority granted to this court—by substituting a verdict of manslaughter for that of murder, and I would direct that the accused reattend before this court for the imposition of a sentence warranted in law," the judge concluded.

The O'Sullivan Concurrence

"I have not a word to say in criticism of Chief Justice Hewak in this case," O'Sullivan said. "He followed the advice of this court in ruling that the accused's statements after the lawyer's visit were admissible. His charge to the jury on constructive murder was in accord with the law as it was laid down by the highest authorities prior to 1987.

"Yet I feel compelled to join with Mr. Justice Huband in setting aside the verdict of guilty of first degree murder.

"I acknowledge that I was wrong in saying, during the last appeal, that 'the detailed confession and the evidence as to what transpired at the murder scene constitute admissible evidence.'

"The reasoning of Mr. Justice Huband persuades me that this was an incorrect statement. The provisions of the Young Offenders Act are clear, in my opinion, and I should have been more cautious in commenting on matters which were not necessary to our earlier decision to direct a new trial.

"On further reflection, I would go even further than Huband, J.A. and say that all the statements given and gestures made after the visit of the lawyer were inadmissible as being involuntary. At common law, and *a fortiori* under the charter, I do not think it was proper for the police to subject this juvenile to interrogation once they knew that he had been advised by counsel not to make statements. This young man was arrested and held in custody for hour on hour and was subjected to a cross-examinatory interrogation which, in my opinion, exceeded the bounds of propriety. Such conduct on the part of the police, in my opinion, tends to bring the judicial system into disrepute.

"If we want to live in a state where the guilty are always punished regardless of the violation of their right to be silent, well and good. I am able to administer law in such a system without problem. But I think it is not sound for us to proclaim the right not to incriminate oneself and yet fail to acknowledge a violation of the right in the case of this 17-year-old boy who, perhaps because of his lack of intelligence, education and spirit, could not have understood and appreciated the warnings of his counsel of his right to 'keep his mouth shut.'"

So often in distress I would turn to the Scriptures for comfort. The mindless criticism of the police, so ill-conceived and unjust, had angered me; the concessions to the killer's supposed naïveté had appalled me.

But I found solace in that portion of Ecclesiastes that is concerned with wisdom and folly, and where it is written: "The beginning of the words of his mouth is foolishness: and the end of his talk is mischievous madness."[2]

The Monnin Dissent

Alfred Monnin had succeeded the revered Samuel Freedman as the province's chief justice in 1983. At the time he wrote his dissenting judgment in R. v. John Thomas James Jr. (No. 2), he had been sitting as a superior court judge for 27 years.

There was an almost Trumanesque slant to the pen of this urbane and erudite jurist. He had always eschewed the florid phrases of some of his judicial brethren, preferring sentences constructed with good, garden-variety English.

But latterly, I had come to realize, his lordship was indulging in some marvellous pugilistic prose.

"The purpose of the charter," he wrote, "was, I believe, to set down in writing, rights which for years had been recognized under common law and fundamental principles of justice in our Canadian democracy. The charter was not proclaimed in a vacuum. Prior to 1982, Canada was, as it is now, a free and democratic country. Citizens had rights which had hitherto been established by common law—a system we inherited from England—by statute law and by judicial pronouncements. The charter, in certain instances, has created new rights. But the purpose of the charter, which must not be forgotten, was to enshrine, in writing, existing rights. To read into Section 7 [the right to life, liberty and the security of the person and the right not to be deprived thereof except in accordance with the principles of fundamental justice] and Section 10(b) [the right to retain and instruct counsel without delay and to be informed of that right] the right to stop all interrogation by investigating officers the moment legal counsel has been retained and has visited and spoken to an accused is to read into those two sections what is plainly not written in them and to read in them that which does not necessarily flow therefrom.

"The charter was not meant as an instrument to hinder the work of police officers nor a curtailment of their duties and functions. Its purpose was to give or confirm rights to individuals. The right to life, liberty and security of an individual has nothing to do with the duty of police officers to properly investigate cases which have been assigned to them. An individual, upon arrest and/or detention—in this case the young person was both arrested and detained—has the right to retain and instruct counsel without delay and to be informed of that right. In the case before us, the accused was promptly informed of his rights by the police officers. They desisted from questioning him until Ms.

Keyser arrived. She spent more than half an hour with her client and she had ample time to advise him of his rights and to request that he accept instructions from her. Obviously, when he was told to remain silent, he was free to accept that advice or to ignore it. There is no right given to counsel to instruct police officers to refrain from questioning their client unless it is done in his or her presence. Some maintain that it is an illusory right if police officers, moments after counsel has left the detention cell or interview room, can immediately continue their interrogation. I must confess that this argument has no appeal for me and holds no sway. The right to remain silent is there—it has existed for many centuries under English law. The accused can choose to remain mute or to talk. If he is a rather weak-willed individual who, after having been told to keep his mouth shut, succumbs to the temptation to answer questions and gives a full account of the events—whether the statement is exculpatory or inculpatory—that is his right and his responsibility alone. The task of law enforcement is arduous and difficult enough without asking police officers to act as baby-sitters.

"Where I disagree with my colleague Huband," Monnin wrote, "is when he rhetorically asks: 'But guilt as to what crime?' and then goes on to discuss Vaillancourt and its effect which leads him to conclude that a verdict of manslaughter, not murder, is the appropriate verdict in this case.

"The accused was charged with first degree murder in that the death was caused by him while committing or attempting to commit a sexual assault upon the victim. The Criminal Code states that culpable homicide is murder where a person causes the death of a human being while committing or attempting to commit sexual acts whether or not he means to cause death to any human being, or whether or not he knows that death is likely to be caused to any human being if he means to cause bodily harm for the purpose of facilitating the commission of the offence, i.e., sexual assault. To strike a three-year-old child with a 50-pound cinder block is certainly to mean to cause bodily harm to that child. She was crying and screaming for her grandmother and the accused wanted to silence her. As well, there is no doubt that the child was sexually assaulted.

"Irrespective of whether a murder is planned and deliberate on the part of any person, murder is first degree murder in respect of a person when the death is caused by that person while committing or attempting to commit sexual assault."

The chief justice was critical of his colleagues for having substituted a verdict of manslaughter on the basis of the alleged unconstitutionality of that section of the Criminal Code under which the accused had been charged.

"It would appear," he observed, "that many Canadian judges are keen on the charter and some courts may be inclined to flex their judicial muscles a little too easily and too often under these new-found powers. It may very well be that, at some later date, the nine members of the Supreme Court will, with great ease, declare the section [213(a)] to be inoperative because it infringes on the charter. But if it is done, it will be done after a full hearing on the issues and with the participation of both the federal and provincial Crown.

"I do not think that it is the duty of a portion only of a provincial appellate tribunal so to do when the issue was not even raised by counsel or properly canvassed and without the intervention of the federal Crown. I am of the view that there has not been an infringement of the charter or that there has not been a sufficient breach of the Young Offenders Act to warrant a review of the second verdict."

Monnin held that the charge of manslaughter (that is, the unintentional killing of a human being) was not consistent with the facts of the case.

"By a majority of two to one, this court told Madam Justice Krindle that she was wrong on all counts. It then stated that the detailed confession and the evidence as to what transpired at the murder scene constituted admissible evidence. At the second trial, Chief Justice Hewak carefully followed this directive. Now he is to be told that the court erred and that there was a breach of the Young Offenders Act and that the proper verdict is not first degree murder but manslaughter. One can only wonder at the conflicting directions and mixed signals lower court judges are receiving from this tribunal. The factual situation is clear. There was a killing and the author of it was the accused.

Two jury panels reached that conclusion without difficulty. In addition to that, we have the voluntary statement of the young person admitting that he committed the crime. To reach any other conclusion but that of guilty of murder is to ignore the real facts of this case."

Monday, February 8, 1988

I walked listlessly through the marbled halls of the old Law Courts Building, nagged by a foreboding in the pit of my stomach. I was making my way toward the Court of Appeal where little Ruby's killer was about to be sentenced.

Appellate court judges constantly hear appeals against sentences meted out in the trial courts. This was the first time in my memory, however, that the Court of Appeal was about to impose sentence as if it were a court of first instance.

Two of the three members who were sitting that morning had not served their apprenticeships in the trial division, but had been appointed directly to the Court of Appeal. I wondered, resentfully, what the devil they knew about sentencing.

"We will hear your submission as to sentence," Monnin announced tonelessly as he glanced in the direction of the three Crown counsel seated to his left.

I reminded myself that the prisoner was about to be sentenced for manslaughter. I must be cautious. I carefully reviewed the evidence surrounding the killing of the child.

"Her life was snuffed out by one intent upon gratifying his vile sexual lust," I pleaded passionately. "He killed the child to avoid detection."

"You are now arguing the intent to kill her," O'Sullivan spat back, cautioning me that this and other statements I had made bordered on contempt of court.

"That's another case. When the Supreme Court hears it, it may well be back to a sentence of murder," he sneered. "I think you are being contemptuous."

An electric current passed through my body as I listened in shock and utter disbelief to this unwarranted insult. I stepped from the lectern and raised my arms in a gesture of near helplessness. My voice was calm, but my temples were pounding.

"My lord, I don't think I have ever been contemptuous of a court for a day in my life; indeed, not even for a minute."

Abruptly, I returned to the lectern to finish my task.

"No punishment that this court may impose will ever atone for this vicious, savage crime.

"Justice cries out—justice demands—the maximum penalty for this atrocity—imprisonment for life!"

Huband asked if a life sentence was regarded as more serious than any fixed term of 30 or 40 years.

"I don't know, my lord," I replied.

That prompted another serpent-tongued retort from O'Sullivan.

"You ask us to impose the most severe sentence. I'm entitled to ask what the most severe is."

As I sat down again, I looked up at the scowling jurist and found solace in the realization that "the words of a wise man's mouth are gracious; but the lips of a fool will swallow up himself."[3]

Keyser made her submission on behalf of the prisoner; then the panel retired to decide upon a fit and proper sentence. As if it were preordained, however, court resumed before the pipe was nicely lit.

"We impose upon this accused a term of 24 years in the penitentiary for this particular offence of manslaughter," Monnin announced dispassionately.

Kim Adriaenssens had listened numbly to the bartering over the number of years the prisoner should spend in custody in exchange for her daughter's life.

She slipped out of the gallery, gaunt and crushed. I awaited her in the corridor. I pressed her arm and she gripped my hands in hers. She tried in vain to smile. There was nothing more to say.

I could never know the weight of the cross she had to bear. No loved one of mine had ever been murdered. And yet, the pain I felt for her was very real.

I walked by the tall oak doors through which I had passed so often with pride, respect, even reverence.

This day it had become a doorway to despair, disgust, and, yes, perhaps even contempt.

CHAPTER 18

"The issue of a juvenile's rights—especially when a juvenile faces a murder charge—is an important one that must be cleared up by the courts once and for all. But that question should never be allowed to overshadow the enormity of James's crime."
—*Winnipeg Sun*, February 10, 1988

Ruby's Rights

The *Winnipeg Sun* editorial that morning was neatly captioned "Legal Niceties Obscure Crime" and was composed with rare insight. It said, in part:

"From the beginning, James's case has been the classic one of a clear-cut, horrible crime becoming inexorably mired in legal technicality.

"It is the sort of case that infuriates anyone who doesn't have the mind of a lawyer.

"We can understand that James, at the time of the crime, was a juvenile. We can understand that he had been arrested and held by police for several hours, and he probably felt frightened.

"But in all the controversy over James's confession, no one has ever claimed the police beat him up or made up the words in which he gave details of the brutal killing.

"In fact, police originally thought James was a witness, until he came out with a bogus story blaming someone else as the killer. Later, he confessed.

"From the beginning, those statements drove judges, police and lawyers around one legal bend after another. Should James have had a lawyer present? Should he have had an adult guardian as well?

"Those questions have flummoxed every judge who has dealt with them. But they didn't seem to bother the two juries who found James guilty of murder.

"The average person finds it hard to believe that a legal technicality could overshadow such a terrible crime. Still, the court battle over James's rights as a juvenile rages on, and he may yet be set free."

It was a bitter March afternoon. Charcoal snow-clouds were releasing torrents of white pellets that exploded as a savage north wind threw them against the window glass.

"Mr. Swanson is here to see you, sir. He doesn't have an appointment."

"Mr. Swanson doesn't believe in making appointments, Barbara. Please show him in."

The visitor shed flakes of melting snow as he entered my office. Droplets of water rolled down his rose-coloured cheeks. He clutched a bulging Canada Safeway bag in his left hand while extending his right, like a large paw, in greeting. Then, having deposited the bag in the middle of my desk, he slumped onto the couch without saying a word.

Bill Swanson was the kindly caretaker of the Inglis Block. He was the keeper of what had been Ruby Adriaenssens' enchanted castle, the place where she danced in the sunbeams, lived out her fairy-tales, and played with the other children who were in the block.

Sometimes, Swanson joined in their games of hide-and-seek. Other times, he played catch with them in the hallways. He didn't get mad when they rode their tricycles along the floors. He was the candy-man, while his wife, "Aunty Marlene," supplied lots of cookies.

"This is no day for man or beast to be outside. What brings you down here, Bill?" I asked.

The interloper still said nothing, but instead pointed his right index finger at his mysterious plump parcel.

He was a good-sized man, strongly built, with long, sloping shoulders and a deep, broad chest. His brown eyes were small and set wide apart. His ears were high on his head, wide and not at all large. His face had reddish-brown markings. Overall, his appearance evoked a kind of shaggy nobility.

He had a balanced temperament and a love for young children. It was this trait, this particular love for little people, that had propelled him towards the justice building on that ferocious winter day.

"I loved that little kid," Swanson had been heard to say on more than one occasion, his eyes filling with tears as he spoke of Ruby. "I can't stop thinking about what was happening to her before John James killed her."

He removed a dog-eared, outdated copy of the Canadian Charter of Rights and Freedoms from his bag.

"Listen to this," he said. "I want you to hear something."

Until my own day of judgment, I will see the bedraggled Swanson clearly, clinging to the charter as the preacher clings to the Word. And I will hear the scornful rasp in the throat of that unofficial spokesperson for citizens who feel betrayed by judges and lawyers who worship at the charter's shrine.

"Section 7! Everyone has the right to life, liberty and the security of the person. What about little Ruby's right to life, goddamnit?" he seethed.

"Section 15! Every individual is equal before and under the law and has the right to the equal protection and equal benefit of the law. What about little Ruby's rights to equal protection and benefit of the law?"

His flailing fingers found the Young Offenders Act. He flipped the pages to Section 56.

"What a sham," he scoffed. "It makes us the laughing-stock of the civilized world."

He became more agitated.

"I'll tell you what it does. It shields young punks from criminal responsibility while literally de-nutting the police."

Swanson upended the bag and scores of letters cascaded into a pile. Letter upon letter denounced the appeal court's second decision, spoke of profound disillusionment with the justice system and called for reinstatement of the death penalty for murder—letters from parents and grandparents, from exasperated taxpayers, even one from six inmates of a neighbouring penal institution.

"If there was ever a case that would justify the return of the death penalty," said one writer, "the brutal murder of little Ruby is just that case."

Another cried:

"I can't conceive of how this proven, cold-blooded murderer and rapist of an innocent three-year-old has any rights left whatsoever. When he committed these acts, he gave up any and all rights to be treated as a human being. The simple fact is that he showed no consideration for Ruby or her rights. Why should we be so concerned with his?

"Our Charter of Rights was supposed to protect the innocent. It is too bad that the lawyers and some judges can't seem to remember that above all else."

Yet another correspondent expressed similar views:

"Why is it that legal technicalities always favour the criminal and never the victim?

"As a taxpayer of many years, I resent, more and more, the use of technicalities in the defence of these social misfits. As a law-abiding citizen and sometime believer in our system of justice, I am now beginning to note the plus side of vigilante groups.

"The reinstatement of a first degree murder charge is still lenient in this instance."

And from one of the prison inmates:

"I would like to see the death penalty imposed. He, John James, is guilty of first degree murder, nothing else."

The words "FIRST DEGREE MURDER" were written in letters three-quarters of an inch high.

In a postscript, a different con concluded that "the justice system made a major mistake. This is giving every murderer a free shot to kill someone."

Swanson solemnly reassembled his makeshift plastic portfolio and presented it to me. He had an abiding conviction that once the judges of the Supreme Court of Canada had read the letters, there would be an automatic restoration of the first degree murder verdict.

"You've got to show these letters to the judges in the Supreme Court," he implored. "They've got to know how the people feel."

Alas, the judges would never see the mass of letters collected by the concerned man with the big heart. They just weren't relevant.

The Swanson papers will never be housed in the National Archives nor in the Parliamentary Library. Lost to legal scholars and historians is a rich source of anecdotal material so vital to an understanding and appreciation of the nosedive taken by the Canadian justice system since the advent of the charter.

I read and reread the written expressions of shocked disbelief and profound condemnation. They demonstrated, in microcosm, a universal uneasiness and growing impatience with a justice system sorely in need of a complete revamping; a system which, for most Canadians, had fallen into disrepute. As well, a palpable smouldering resentment for a decayed national parole service was very much in evidence.

The paramount revelation to be gleaned from the papers was simply this: An overwhelming number of outraged Canadians were on the verge of demanding the return of the death penalty in appropriate cases. Others, who were opposed to capital punishment, insisted that there no longer be parole for those convicted of first degree murder.

A secondary revelation emerging from the pens of the disenchanted citizens was the scathing condemnation of criminal lawyers in general and John James's lawyer in particular.

One lady, whose decorative hand and scented, daintily patterned paper belied her feelings, wrote:

"I agree that John James should be strung up at high noon

to die a long and agonizing death in the city square—but not without his lawyer swinging there beside him."

Valerie, young and angry, expressed her disillusionment in her prefatory line: "Justice, if there is such a thing—"

And then: "I want John James to be executed or to remain in prison for the rest of his days."

So did 96 fellow citizens whom she had single-handedly canvassed; 96 signatures appended to her writing bore witness to this fact.

An irate grandmother expressed another recurring issue when she complained that "the criminal will be fed and clothed, entertained and educated at taxpayers' expense."

There clearly was a slow-burning resentment in the breasts of those destined to foot the bill for mollycoddled convicts.

Bill Swanson's correspondents were, by and large, thoughtful, caring people. They poured out sympathy for the Adriaenssens family and grief over Ruby's murder. And they were united in another common theme so eloquently expressed by a 19-year-old youth.

"The Charter of Rights and Freedoms is of undeniable importance, but its application must be for justice first."

The bulging Safeway bag stored in one of my file cabinets may be but an impotent reminder of Bill Swanson's folly. But, it is a lasting memorial to a rare and good man, the kindly caretaker who took the time to care.

CHAPTER 19

"Ordering a new trial would, in my view,
subvert the interests of the justice system...."
—Madam Justice C. L'Heureux-Dubé, 1990

The Supreme Court Judgment

September 13, 1990. Five years to the day that James killed Ruby.

By a majority of six to one, the Supreme Court of Canada confirmed that John Thomas James Jr. would stand trial again— but this time, for manslaughter.

Among its conclusions, the court ruled that all of the key statements James made to police were inadmissible under the terms of Section 56 of the Young Offenders Act.

Writing for the majority, Mr. Justice Peter Cory noted:

"Parliament has recognized the problems and difficulties that beset young people when confronted with authority. It may be unnecessary and frustrating to the police and society that a worldly-wise, smug 17-year-old with apparent anti-social tendencies should derive the benefit of this section. Yet it must be remembered that the section is to protect all young people of 17 years or less."

It was obvious that the eminent jurist had reflected long upon James's emotional and physical condition at the time of his interrogation. He clearly had not visualized the young killer as the naïve, ill-educated, frightened boy conjured up in the mind of Joseph Francis O'Sullivan. Neither would he accept the portrait that the prosecutors had tried to paint of an unrepentant, lying, dangerous, streetwise punk.

"No matter how worldly-wise John Thomas James may have been," Cory wrote, "by the time of his second statement he must have been a tired 17-year-old after spending nearly seven hours in police custody."

There was some solace to be found in the dissenting judgment of Madam Justice L'Heureux-Dubé. She, however, did not prevail.

Prior to the offence, she wrote, James "had lived in a common-law relationship for about 10 months. That union produced a child. While he no longer resides with the mother, he had made sporadic support payments. John Thomas James was working as a roofer for his cousin Harry James, who was present at the police station and provided guidance and support. When the police advised him of his right to counsel, James produced a solicitor's business card from his pocket. He subsequently consulted with his solicitor for 37 minutes. The solicitor either acknowledged the police's statement that they would have to speak to John Thomas James some more, or told the police that her client would not be making a statement.

"These facts reveal that the accused was relatively advanced and well apprised of his predicament. His level of maturity would have alerted him to the dangers of answering certain questions after he had received explicit warnings from both the police as well as his solicitor. These indicia of adulthood do not excuse non-compliance with the act. Rather, they define with sharper resolution what measures are necessary in order to extend the prescribed safeguards to this particular young person, taking into account his age and level of sophistication.

"The Young Offenders Act ensures that the rights of young persons are upheld by extending to them additional safeguards that must be adhered to. The barometer of adherence must be calibrated according to the particular youth, having regard to all of the surrounding factors and circumstances. Ordering a third trial would, in my view, subvert the interests of the justice system and the protection of our youths. Respect for the act can

only be preserved through logical application. Uniform imple-
mentation in all cases would ignore the vast range of individuals who fall within the ambit of protection, and thus frustrate
the objectives and purposes of the act itself.

"Furthermore, there *was* compliance in the present case. As
soon as John Thomas James became a suspect, his closest adult
relative in Winnipeg was brought to the Public Safety Building.
John Thomas James was granted and exercised his right to retain and instruct counsel. Following consultation with both of
these individuals, John Thomas James made incriminating statements voluntarily, on the basis of which he was convicted of
first degree murder twice. The procedural requirements dictated
by the act were observed, and, in my view, ordering a third trial
would severely undermine rather than preserve the utility of
the Young Offenders Act.

"I would allow the appeal, dismiss the cross-appeal, and
restore the conviction and sentence imposed at trial."

CHAPTER 20

Trial No. 3: December 10, 1990

With the exception of the indefatigable Brenda Keyser, fresh faces appeared at counsel table as James's manslaughter trial opened before Mr. Justice Theodore Glowacki. The judge was, by coincidence, the third sometime-Crown attorney to preside at one of the child-killer's trials.

Richard Saull carried the ball for the prosecution. Extremely bright, a little arrogant perhaps, a deadly prosecutor whom any criminal would prefer to avoid, Saull brought to mind the image of the muscular little figure on a Baby Ruth candy-bar wrapper.

Les Kee had put his barrister's robe in mothballs on January 22, 1988, the day Huband and O'Sullivan adjudged James guilty, not of murder in the first degree, but of the lesser crime of manslaughter. Another good Crown attorney had lost his ardour for the practice of criminal law. The focus of Kee's work in the department subsequently changed. He also began to plan actively for a third career as a carefree fishing guide, piloting American anglers to churning waters teeming with pickerel, pike and walleye.

Drew Baragar was not at the defence table. He had died on February 17, 1988, a day that counsel sorrowfully remember. Road conditions were treacherous as Baragar set out early for the juvenile court complex. Icy patches impaired the asphalt surface along Kenaston Boulevard. His sports car went into a skid and out of control. He passed away in hospital without regaining consciousness. For this slight, amiable, promising young lawyer, life's journey had been all too short.

On December 19, after just three hours of deliberation, the jury found John James Jr. guilty of manslaughter as charged.

Two days later, he was consigned to the penitentiary for 22 years.

Keyser filed a notice of appeal on January 14, 1991, contending that the sentence was "harsh and excessive, having regard to the circumstances of the offence, the background of the accused, and the previous sentence imposed."

On June 11, the Court of Appeal set aside the 22-year term and replaced it with a life sentence.

The irrepressible Keyser was readily accessible when Terry Weber of the *Winnipeg Free Press* came to call.

"This is it," she said. "There's no avenue of appeal from this."

Weber went on to tell readers that:

"Although the Appeal Court ruling technically increased the sentence, Keyser said the decision is beneficial to her client because he will be eligible for parole by September, 1992, sooner than if the previous sentence had been upheld.

"Those sentenced to life imprisonment on charges that do not specify how much time must be served before they can apply for parole automatically become eligible after serving seven years.

"Keyser said yesterday's sentence takes into account the five-and-a-half years James has served in prison before the most recent sentence was imposed.

"That period was not taken into consideration when the last sentence was handed down."[1]

Thus it was that we had bartered the life of a beautiful child for a paltry seven years.

As I raised my eyes from the newspaper, I silently cursed the killer and his counsel and all those who had tampered with the scales of justice.

"Has John Thomas James Jr. been released from prison?"

"How much pen time did he do?"

"Where is he now?"

"What restrictions have been placed on his activities?"

It was impossible to pry the answers to these and other questions from officials in the employ of the Correctional Service of Canada. Such disclosure, they said, would fly in the face of certain strictures laid down in the Privacy Act and the Corrections and Conditional Release Act, two statutes of the Parliament of Canada.

This bureaucratic reticence left me with the distinct impression that any such disclosure would, in the minds of those servants of the solicitor general of Canada, impair the very security of this nation.

Ordinarily, I would simply have picked up the telephone and learned of the prisoner's release date from his or her counsel. In the instant matter, however, this was not to be. Brenda Keyser no longer acts for John Thomas James Jr. She was appointed to the Court of Queen's Bench on the 3rd day of October, 1995, as one of Her Majesty's justices.

Thus, I have been unable to respond intelligibly to the incessant callers demanding information as to the convicted killer's whereabouts.

I continue to mull over the so-called rights of the criminal afforded to him upon his release from prison. I brood about his right to privacy and his right to anonymity.

I decry the naïveté of those lawmakers whose folly can only lead to increased recidivism.

The fathers and mothers of all precious, vulnerable children are entitled to know the release dates and whereabouts of predatory pedophiles.

It is my fervent hope that we have the good sense to strive for reformation.

Mr. Justice Gordon Hall
October 25, 1990

Mr. Justice Joseph O'Sullivan
December 16, 1992

Chief Justice Samuel Freedman
March 6, 1993

Declaration of Principle

3. (1) Policy for Canada with Respect to Young Offenders
—It is hereby recognized and declared that

(a) crime prevention is essential to the long-term protection of society and requires addressing the underlying causes of crime by young persons and developing multi-disciplinary approaches to identifying and effectively responding to children and young persons at risk of committing offending behaviour in the future;

(a.1) while young persons should not in all instances be held accountable in the same manner or suffer the same consequences for their behaviour as adults, young persons who commit offences should nonetheless bear responsibility for their contraventions;

(b) society must, although it has the responsibility to take reasonable measures to prevent criminal conduct by young persons, be afforded the necessary protection from illegal behaviour;

(c) young persons who commit offences require supervision, discipline and control, but, because of their state of dependency and level of development and maturity, they also have special needs and require guidance and assistance;

(c.1) the protection of society, which is a primary objective of the criminal law applicable to youth, is best served by rehabilitation, wherever possible, of young persons who commit offences, and rehabilitation is best achieved by addressing the needs and circumstances of a young person that are relevant to the young person's offending behaviour;

(d) where it is not inconsistent with the protection of society, taking no measures or taking measures other than judicial proceedings under this Act should be considered for dealing with young persons who have committed offences;

(e) young persons have rights and freedoms in their own right, including those stated in the *Canadian Charter of Rights and Freedoms* or in the *Canadian Bill of Rights*, and in particular a right to be heard in the course of, and to participate in, the processes that lead to decisions that affect them, and young persons should have special guarantees of their rights and freedoms;

(f) in the application of this Act, the rights and freedoms of young persons include a right to the least possible interference with freedom that is consistent with the protection of society, having regard to the needs of young persons and the interests of their families;

(g) young persons have the right, in every instance where they have rights and freedoms that may be affected by this Act, to be informed as to what those rights and freedoms are; and

(h) parents have responsibility for the care and supervision of their children, and, for that reason, young persons should be removed from parental supervision either partly or entirely only when measures that provide for continuing parental supervision are inappropriate.

Section 56 of the
Young Offenders Act

56 (1) Subject to this section, the law relating to the admissibility of statements made by persons accused of committing offences applies in respect of young persons.

    (2) No oral or written statement given by a young person to a peace officer or other person who is, in law, a person in authority is admissible against the young person unless

    (a) the statement was voluntary;

    (b) the person to whom the statement was given has, before the statement was made, clearly explained to the young person, in language appropriate to his age and understanding, that

        (i) the young person is under no obligation to give a statement,

        (ii) any statement given by him may be used as evidence in proceedings against him,

        (iii) the young person has the right to consult another person in accordance with paragraph (c), and

        (iv) any statement made by the young person is required to be made in the presence of the person consulted, unless the young person desires otherwise;

(c)   the young person has, before the statement was made, been given a reasonable opportunity to consult with counsel or a parent, or in the absence of a parent, an adult relative, or in the absence of a parent and an adult relative, any other appropriate adult chosen by the young person; and

(d)   where the young person consults any person pursuant to paragraph (c), the young person has been given a reasonable opportunity to make the statement in the presence of that person.

(3)   The requirements set out in paragraphs (2)(b), (c) and (d) do not apply in respect of oral statements where they are made spontaneously by the young person to a peace officer or other person in authority before that person has had a reasonable opportunity to comply with those requirements.

(4)   A young person may waive his rights under paragraph (2)(c) or (d) but any such waiver shall be made in writing and shall contain a statement signed by the young person that he has been apprised of the right that he is waiving.

(5)   A youth court judge may rule inadmissible in any proceedings under this Act a statement given by the young person in respect of whom the proceedings are taken if the young person satisfies the judge that the statement was given under duress imposed by any person who is not, in law, a person in authority.

(6)   For the purpose of this section, an adult consulted pursuant to paragraph 56(2)(c) shall, in the absence of evidence to the contrary, be deemed not to be a person in authority.

Chapter 2 1. *The Holy Bible*, The Gospel According to St. Matthew, Chapters 5–7.
    7 1. *Winnipeg Sun*, March 11, 1986.
      2. Boucher v. The Queen, 1955 *Supreme Court of Canada Reports*, p. 23.
      3. *Winnipeg Free Press*, March 11, 1986.
      4. *Winnipeg Sun*, March 11, 1986.
      5. Ibid.
      6. Ibid.
      7. *Winnipeg Free Press*, March 11, 1986.
    8 1. *Winnipeg Free Press*, March 12, 1986.
    9 1. Alfred Allan Lewis, *The Evidence Never Lies* (New York: Holt, Rinehart and Winston, 1984).
    10 1. Richard Fountain, *The Wit of the Wig* (London: Leslie Frewin, 1968).
    13 1. *Winnipeg Sun*, May 2, 1986.
      2. *Winnipeg Free Press*, May 2, 1986.
    14 1. *Winnipeg Free Press*, November 28, 1986.
    15 1. Georg A. Brongers and Tiemen H. Kimm, *Nicotiana Tabacum*, Trans. W.C. Ter Spill (Groningen: Theodorus Niemeyer N.V., 1964).
      2. Charles Dickens, *Oliver Twist*, (London: Penguin Books, 1966) Chapter 51.
      3. *Winnipeg Sun*, January 18, 1987.
      4. *Winnipeg Free Press*, January 18, 1987.
      5. Mark M. Orkin, *Legal Ethics: A Study of Professional Conduct*, (Toronto: Cartwright and Sons, Ltd., 1957) p. 185.
      6. Mathers, *C.L. Times* 809.
    16 1. *Winnipeg Free Press*, May 1, 1987.
      2. *Winnipeg Sun*, May 1, 1987.
    17 1. Edmund Burke, "Letters on a Regicide Peace." In *Selected Works*, ed. E.J. Payne.
      2. *The Holy Bible*, Ecclesiastes, Chapter 10:13.
      3. Ibid, 10:12.
    20 1. *Winnipeg Free Press*, June 12, 1991.

A

B
Baragar, Drew, 78, 99, 181, 186, 212
Bellingham, Sgt. Wayne, 23-24, 41-42, 88, 103
Boan, Cst. Craig, 24, 25, 40-42, 51-52, 112
    as witness, 81-82
Bowman, Sterling M., 94
Burke, Edmund, 187

C
Cadieux, James Ernest, 42, 58-59, 88, 149
    defence view of his testimony, 121-25
    judge's view of testimony, 136-37
    testimony, 101-6
Carmelo, 18
Chesterton, Gilbert K., 73, 190
Chitty, Lord Justice, 98
Coleman, Ronald, 163
Conner, Judge Arnold, 50, 67
    discharges James, 53-60, 64-65
Cory, Mr. Justice Peter, 209-10
Courchene, Eva, 95, 130, 142, 143, 148
Cox, Bob, 160, 165

D
Demas, Corrine Marie, 30, 31-33, 34, 35, 82, 94, 95, 96, 111, 112, 114, 115, 117, 119, 125, 129-130, 131, 133, 142, 143
Devries, Cst. Bruce, 24, 25, 40-41
Dewar, Q.C., Archibald S. (later Chief Justice), 158
Dickens, Charles, 171
Dickson, Mr. Justice R.G.B., 163

E
Eliot, George, 68
Ellis, Dr. Eric, 47, 48
Elton, Tanner, 65

F
Freedman, Chief Justice Samuel, 163, 187, 196

G
Gallagher, Q.C., Roy, 62
Gaudette, Barry D., 121-22
Glowacki, Mr. Justice Theodore, 212

Y

John D. (Jack) Montgomery, Q.C. is a former Chief Prosecutor for the City of Winnipeg; Provincial Director of Criminal Prosecutions; and a General Counsel in Manitoba's Department of Justice. Although retired, he is still conscripted to prosecute murderers.